FRODO'S QUEST

FRODO'S QUEST

Living the Myth in
The Lord of the Rings

Robert Ellwood

Quest Books
Theosophical Publishing House

Wheaton, Illinois ♦ Chennai (Madras), India

The Theosophical Society acknowledges with gratitude the generous support of the Kern Foundation for the publication of this book.

The Theosophical Publishing House
P. O. Box 270
Wheaton, Illinois 60189-0270

Cover art composite, book design, and typesetting by Dan Doolin

The images in this book appear by the courtesy of the following artists:

Bonnie Callahan, pp. 11, 14, 105, 118, 128

Anke Eissmann, pp. 92, 99

Michael Green, pp. 1, 8, 17, 18, 26, 31, 35, 48, 50, 55, 64, 67, 82, 87, 89, 90, 94, 97, 104, 122, 127. Reprinted with permission from *A Hobbit's Journal*, Copyright © 1979 by Running Press Book Publishers, Philadelphia and London, www.runningpress.com

Michael Green, pp. 53, 68, 76, 102, 112, 115, 121, 140–141. Reprinted with permission from *A Tolkien Treasury*, Copyright © 2000, 1989, and 1978 by Running Press Book Publishers, Philadelphia and London, www.runningpress.com

Christiaan Iken, pp. 37, 79

Library of Congress Cataloging-in-Publication Data

Ellwood, Robert S.,
Frodo's quest: living the myth in The lord of the rings / Robert Ellwood.
p.   cm.
Includes bibliographical references.
ISBN 0-8356-0823-9
1. Tolkien, J. R. R. (John Ronald Reuel), 1892–1973. Lord of the rings.   2. Fantasy fiction, English—History and criticism.   3. Baggins, Frodo (Fictitious character)   4. Quests (Expeditions) in literature.   5. Middle Earth (Imaginary place)   6. Theosophy in literature.   I. Title.

PR6039.O32 L6324 2002
823'.912—dc21   2002068387

6   5   4   3   2   1   *   02   03   04   05   06   07   08

Printed in the United States of America

Contents

Preface

The numbers in parentheses in this book after quotations or references to J. R. R. Tolkien's *The Lord of the Rings* are to the volume and page number of the original edition (London, 1954–5). A synopsis of the story of *The Hobbit* and *The Lord of the Rings* can be found in appendix A. The present book deals just with those works, and not other related works of the Tolkien canon.

I would like to thank Sharron Dorr, publishing manager of Quest Books and the Theosophical Publishing House, for overall encouragement and support of this project. I would also like to thank Dan Doolin, who was responsible for the wonderful assemblage of Tolkien art presented in *Frodo's Quest*, for his untiring and immensely creative labors on behalf of this project. I am especially grateful to Bonnie Callahan for creating several fine custom works of art for this book. Special thanks also go to Adele Algeo and Ananya Rajan for their editorial assistance and to John Algeo, President of the Theosophical Society in America, who personally took on the task of editing this manuscript, armed with a sure literary eye, deep Theosophical wisdom, and the enthusiasm of a fellow Tolkien fan. Above all I would like to thank my wife, Gracia Fay, who read the chapters of this book as they were written and made innumerable astute suggestions for improvement based on both an incomparable familiarity with the Tolkien text and a former English teacher's sense of clear style. Any remaining flaws in this text are, needless to say, entirely my own.

R.E.

Frodo Baggins

Lands of the Heart

Have you ever visited a perfect place somewhere in the back gardens of your mind where, as in the dreamland of the musical *Camelot*, the sun always shines when we wish it to or where, as in Shangri-La, wise monks contemplate eternal truth far above the world and its wars? Is this secret garden occasionally your refuge for learning and refreshment?

Have you then wandered outside the garden walls on to another, more rugged private landscape, one with a magnificent view of towering peaks and green valleys and perhaps a sea harbor where vessels set sail into otherworldly mists laced with the light of sunrise?

That utopian continent is not free of danger or conflict. In it adventure adds to the spice and splendor of life. Venturing onto its rough terrain, you know that life without moments of intensity and peril would hardly be life on the human plane at all. In that brave world you realize that an existence which does not some day waken to wonder and terror beyond all previous imagining—and does not occasionally face crises that stiffen the muscles and sharpen the gaze—would not be a life in which we could become all we can be.

All those vistas are found in Middle-earth, the world that J. R. R. Tolkien has given us in *The Lord of the Rings*, his superb epic of crisis and victory in a fabulous world of ages ago. Venturing into its Elven realms, one finds beauty keener than grief, beauty made all the more poignant by knowledge that the roots of the Elf race reach very deep into the mythic past, but that the time of their kindred is coming to an end, and the Elves are leaving Middle-earth for the timeless remembering and joy of the eternal Elvenhome across the Sundering Sea. In the Hobbits, almost more than in the heroic-scale men of Middle-earth, we see ourselves: creatures of habit; enjoyers of simple, cozy comforts; full of gossip, yet able to rise to unanticipated levels of courage when occasion summons it forth.

Just as Middle-earth is populated by a diversity of peoples, so it is marked by gradations of good and evil. On the good side, one looks from the sometimes courageous Hobbits to wise Wizards and an Elven queen who is almost a goddess of wisdom. Evil ranges from "ordinary" people (or Hobbits) who compromise themselves too much by scoffing at beauty or scouting everyday fair dealing, to the Dark Lord himself—Sauron, the Eye of Mordor. He lives only for power and strives always to increase his slave domain through force, but above all through fear.

The Dark Lord's power is lodged mainly in a Ring of evil magic, which has come into the hands of the Hobbit Frodo. That unlikely middle-aged hero knows that he must take the Ring to the Cracks of Doom in the Land of Mordor, where it was made, in order to destroy it. Frodo, who like most of us would much prefer to stay home and enjoy an easy life, must steel himself to accomplish that exceedingly dangerous mission. In the process of carrying out his mission, he finds that he learns much about both himself and the world that is little known to those who only stay home, and he passes through experiences that can rightly be regarded as initiations.

Sauron, the Eye of Mordor

The story is magnificent, but is it true? This tale is certainly not something that actually happened in any past age of our particular planet. It might have occurred in some alternative universe, if it is true that an infinite number of other universes exist in infinite space and time, and therefore every possible variation of reality, including even variant physical laws, finds its manifestation somewhere. But if so, we can know nothing of that other universe, for our perception cannot trespass beyond the "Ring-Pass-Not" of our space-time-light continuum.

Here, however, is another way to look at the truth of the story. What moves us deeply in *The Lord of the Rings*, but we think is only fantasy, may after all be more factual than we are aware. Not as history, but as a description of the many planes on which the human spirit lives, the novel may show us more reality than our stay-in-the-Shire neighbors could ever imagine is out there—even more reality than some may want to know.

Try therefore speculating that *The Lord of the Rings* is not fantasy at all in the profoundest sense, but sober truth about the many worlds around us all the time. Set amid realms of silver-white and Ringwraith black and all the other colors of the spectrum, its narrative then becomes an ongoing adventure tale with each of us as the central character. Its veracity is a matter of how deeply we look into the nature of our lives and into all the back gardens and vast continents of consciousness. It may have to do with how far back we trace our lineage—not biological lineage, but karmic and consciousness lineage—and how seriously we take the initiations that we, like Frodo in *The Lord of the Rings*, must undergo before we set sail from the Grey Havens.

In this book, our endeavor will be to slip *The Lord of the Rings* into several of the various levels of reality within which we live, move, and have our being. That will mean opening our eyes to a worldview often described as the Ancient Wisdom. The wide-ranging perspectives of that lore, under a thousand names and forms, was broadly common to humanity before modern times. It still has considerable power, and certainly influenced Tolkien in countless ways. In one of that old knowledge's contemporary expressions, the Ancient Wisdom is called Theosophy, a name by which it will sometimes be identified here.

In the light of the Ancient Wisdom and Theosophy, some of us may catch on to *how* the epic is true, or can be true, here and now in this life—if we go far enough beneath the surface. Exploring at a deep enough level, we track the roots of present-day events ever farther back, until we find they can reach very far indeed into the misty past. Shining the light of deep Wisdom this way and that, we find—adjoining our everyday consciousness—wonders worthy of Lothlórien and all the horrors of Mordor. We espy Wizards and Rangers meeting us on the street, but usually anonymously, until our vision, trained by Wisdom, pierces their masks.

Above all, in this deep-level perception, we see our own lives as more than dreary rounds of one thing after another. Instead, each lifetime becomes a great journey, a pilgrimage, a quest, a mission—and part of an even vaster trek that involves the crossing of many Sundering Seas. *The Lord of the Rings* invites us to reflect on its story, and then to look around us, and to look within ourselves, and to look ahead to plan our own life's next adventures.

But, like Bilbo writing his account called *There and Back Again*, or Frodo setting out on his quest, we need to begin where we are. The greatest myths and epics must start amid the comedy and poignancy of ordinary human life, with ordinary people in ordinary places. We begin in the Shire.

by callahan 2002

Starting Out in the Shire

The great journey to destroy the Ring sets out from the Shire, home of the Hobbits. They are an ordinary folk, with everyday virtues and vices, sorrows and pleasures. They work hard (for the most part), and after a solid day in the fields or the mill, the menfolk enjoy a pint of good brew in the local pub, like any British workingman. The Shire, in fact, is clearly based on a rather idealized picture of the English village and countryside, with their diversity of interesting characters.

So it is that many types of Hobbits dwell in the small universe of the Shire. Frodo is perpetually plagued by the Sackville-Bagginses, who covet his fine home, Bag End. Sam instinctively dislikes Sandyman the miller, a debunker who continually pours cold water on his tenuous yearning for the sight of Elves and beauty beyond the level of his garden. The Shire also houses good honest folk like the Gaffer, Sam's father, and Frodo's lively young cousins, Merry and Pippin, who quip with one another in a manner reminiscent of English schoolboy novels popular in Tolkien's day.

Into this quiet world bursts Bilbo's "long-expected party." That festival day is to commemorate the birthday when he becomes "eleventy-one" (that is, 111 years old), and it coincides with the thirty-third birthday and coming of age of his ward, Frodo. Practically everyone in the neighborhood, and some Hobbits from farther away, receive an invitation. A few are overlooked by accident, but since they come anyway that doesn't matter. The party is really a daylong variety of entertainments, songs, dances, music, games, and in the evening excellent fireworks provided by Gandalf the Wizard. Above all it "snowed food and rained drink," as the Hobbits like to say, and the guests, partial to their victuals like all their kind and not adverse to a convivial glass, are well pleased.

The climax of the party is Bilbo's after-dinner speech. The Hobbit guests are expecting the conventional address, hopefully brief, which the occasion calls for, and that is how it begins. But then the old Hobbit starts saying unexpected things, like "I don't know half of you half as well as I should like; and I like less than half of you half as well as you deserve." They have to work on this to see if it comes out as a compliment, and are in no mood for such mental gymnastics. Then comes the ANNOUNCEMENT, made in stentorian tones. Bilbo declares that this is the end; he is leaving—NOW.

A flash of light, and when all clears, Bilbo is nowhere to be seen. He has disappeared. After a moment of awestruck silence, all begin talking at once, and the talk does not die down for many days.

As those who have read the story know, Bilbo disappeared by using the magic Ring in his possession since an earlier adventure sixty years before. Among its powers is the ability to render invisible anyone who puts it on—although, as Bilbo and his heir Frodo slowly and painfully learn, there is much more to it than that. Bilbo slips away from the party, leaves his possessions (including, with surprising reluctance at the last moment, the Ring), and departs for Rivendell, the "last homely house," the residence of Elves. He is tired; at the same time the sense of wonder that was awakened long before on his first journey has never entirely left him, and he wants again to see mountains and his friends among the star-blest Elven folk. Frodo takes over Bag End and resides there in comfort until summoned to his own even more perilous and critical adventure, to destroy the Ring Bilbo has given him, now known to be the One Ring, source of the power by which the Dark Lord would be able to enslave Middle-earth.

Bilbo Baggins

⬖

These events are the pattern of our spiritual lives. We begin where we are. Whether in city, town, or countryside, we live lives in which a good part of our energy has to be devoted to meeting everyday needs: making money, fixing meals, shopping, cleaning house, perhaps caring for spouse and children. We are surrounded by all sorts of people who rub us in different ways: the irritating neighbor who plays loud music late at night, the infant (our own or someone else's) who won't stop crying, the coworkers we like and don't like, the hard-driving (and insecure) boss, the one friend we can "really talk to."

And you yourself, as though you had a Shire-moot inside you, are just as varied a picture. Some days you feel good, full of energy and the joy of life; other days you are run-down, tired however much rest you get, even

Chapter Two

Gandalf

depressed. You know your moods: often easy-going, sometimes inexplicably crabby, angry, or filled with vague fears and anxieties. Amid all this you may feel you have little time or energy left for spiritual life. You may (or may not) go to church or temple, and say a few prayers, but that's about it. Like many in the Shire who have heard tales of odd sightings and strange doings, you may inwardly feel a bit skeptical when you hear spectacular claims made for religious faith, or at least you think, "That's not for me."

And yet, there are those moments that seem to break the mold, causing one to ponder. The uncanny exaltation you once felt at seeing a flight of wild geese high in the sky, as though they were about to soar beyond the circles of this world altogether. The time your child was very sick, and therapeutic touch, or some kind of special deeply caring spiritual healing, really seemed to help. The days when queer coincidences and inexplicable "chance" meetings with the right person at the right time seemed to happen. Even the time you would almost swear you saw an Elf or a ghost.

For a long time you may just hold on to the memory of such moments, but do not quite know what to do with them. But then comes something so decisive, such a particular call or unavoidable sign, that even not responding is a response. It would be like a Wizard and thirteen Dwarves coming to Bilbo's round-doored house and rousing him to help them recover a treasure from a dragon, or it would be like Bilbo's second disappearance sixty years later and Frodo's knowing he had to leave home when he learned the true nature of his inherited Ring.

The unexpected call may come entangled in one of those situations on which much more is riding than appears at first glance. Indeed, one may feel almost deceived by karma, fate, or the gods when what seems to be just a tea party turns out to be a life-changing afternoon. So it is with Bilbo's first adventure, recorded in *The Hobbit*. A gentle Hobbit of quiet ways, Bilbo is at his ease in the Shire when Gandalf appears, talking rather vaguely about an adventure; Bilbo invites him the next day to tea.

At the appointed hour there come, one after the other, thirteen Dwarves demanding to be served, and finally the Wizard that Bilbo thought was to be his only guest. The host is more than a little put out, as one can well imagine. But he manages as best he can, and then, toward night, the Dwarf guests begin singing. Their songs are such wistful romances of adventure that the Hobbit begins to be moved. He feels something in himself stir that yearns to leave and become part of such storied deeds.

But what really sways the Hobbit to accept the challenge Gandalf and the Dwarves have prepared for him is quite different. Listening to those melodies is of itself a virtual enchantment, and Bilbo falls into a swoon. Nonetheless, he can still hear the words his Dwarf guests speak after the music stops, and they are not complimentary. Some Dwarves are arguing that one who faints so easily may not be the treasure-burglar they are looking for. This gets the Hobbit's dander up, and he rises insisting that he can do the job. The next morning he is again not sure, but it is then too late to back out—the Dwarves and the Wizard are waiting for him.

This is likely to be the way many of us manage, willingly or not, to confront and then, perhaps even more unwillingly, accept a challenge. We are not all going to be bold knights setting out on a fine morning to seek adventure. We are probably more like Hobbits finding that karma and guidance can maneuver us into changes we do not want to make, but which are for our own ultimate good, as well as the good of the world. Opportunity imposes itself on us; we can't get away from it because it is entangled with various obligations of life; we may succumb to an enchanting moment and then it's too late to back out; we accept only because we don't want to say "No" and look like a wimp—all this is more likely than not to be the way the great quest really begins in our Shire-like lives. Yet, also like Hobbits, we discover that when we can't escape the challenge, we find unexpected courage to meet it.

Those moments of meeting our quest are there. Life happens, and challenges are part of it. The challenge may come in the form of a personal crisis in health, marriage, family, or job. Perhaps it is ultimately a spiritual calling rooted in our unfolding, deep-rooted, cause-and-effect destiny, but taking form in interaction with what's happening in the peopled space around us, and now expressing itself insistently in the form of this crisis. That is how karmic destiny often works.

A door may appear unexpectedly—as unexpectedly as Bilbo's party with the Dwarves—that if opened will set you on a bright path leading to adventure, danger, sacrifice, and the prospect of doing great good. If you start walking down that path, it will take you right out of the life you are now living. You know this, and the prospect is both exciting and scary. Can you really make that much of a change?

You could, for example, be offered the chance to change work, even city of residence, for something far more oriented toward world service or spiritual life than where you are now—but for small remuneration and much giving up of that to which you have become accustomed. If taken, that way may, like Frodo's journey, mean travel to harsh terrain and abiding among folk of strange tongue. It may mean denigration, persecution, even death, from those known and unknown who do not understand the meaning of your labor.

Yet the price to be paid if you do not open that door will be spending the rest of your life knowing that once the door stood before you, and you did *not* open it. And the closed door will mean that the world is still unchanged in one little way that seems to have been your responsibility. What you might have done, large or small, to make that change for the better was not accomplished.

Or the change, the sacrifice, to which you are called may be entirely internal, the door completely within. This conviction is not to be scorned if it is arrived at honestly, with as much self-knowledge as is possible. Internal change, the inner pilgrimage, the adventure of the mind and heart, the interior destruction of the Ring of evil, requires personal discipline and effort comparable to that of the physical adventurer who goes to far places and strange duties. For to remake oneself is to remake a world and is the beginning of the restitution of all things. Not a few persons have outwardly stayed where they are, in their jobs, their families, their home towns—their Shires, so to speak—yet have not only taken the adventure, but have been immense forces for good in that place. For there is no place where suffering cannot be alleviated, free folk protected, and joy spread outward like rolling waves of light.

Possibly lifetimes, even ages, of karmic or long-term cause and effect development have prepared one for this chance to open a door, and to change and grow. In the same way, that moment, and its particular lifetime, is a link in a longer chain preparing one for something even higher in the unimaginable future. But the choice is for each individual: you can go through that door, or you can remain outside convincing yourself that you are content where you are. But you can't really go back to where you were the day before the challenge came, because you will always know.

When the call to leave the Shire is sounded, it will change your way of thinking. No more than Bilbo or Frodo, can you any longer just think like an ordinary Hobbit. Hobbits in the Shire prefer others who are like themselves, and they are suspicious of those who are different. This is a very comfortable feeling for one comfortable with life as it is. But once the call has come and the inner self is awakened, that kind of comfort must be left behind. One thing the Ancient Wisdom always tells us is that life is a pilgrimage, and so keeps moving forward.

You realize deep down that, once you have seen the door, or been visited by a Wizard and thirteen Dwarves, you are *not* entirely like the others in the Shire. It may be kindly, as well as prudent, not to make too much of the difference. But you know the day is coming when you will show Shire folk by some unexpected word or deed that you have a special destiny. You may even sense that some morning you will depart for your own Rivendell.

Perhaps like Frodo, as time goes on and the hour of change creeps up on you, you find yourself, figuratively or literally, sometimes wondering about "wild lands"—particularly in times of yearning and dreaming, like autumn. Visions of exotic places may come into your dreams. You may say to yourself, as did the future Ring-bearer, "Perhaps I shall cross the River myself one day," even though the other half of your mind still replies, "Not yet." You may begin to feel restless and, like the Hobbit, find yourself looking at maps, wondering what lies beyond their edges. Like him, you may even find yourself wandering by yourself more often than before and further afield, as though in anticipation of the climactic day of departure (1:52). None of this is easy, but as Gildor the Elf reminds Frodo, courage may arise when least expected (1:94).

The Shire also favors clear-cut boundaries of place and of mind. The Shire Bounders keep unwanted others out of the Hobbits' congenial land, and the Hobbits like things "laid out fair and square." But you will now see the relativity of such hard and fast lines, realizing that also "something there is that does not love a wall." Even in the Shire, at the edge of vision, so to speak, there are mysteries and hints of something more than the ordinary in Hobbit (or human) life and its cosmic environment: the Ring, old stories, peculiar reports from the frontiers. It is at these intersections that the call comes and the quest begins.

So when we are ready and the summons has sounded, the journey will commence. As Frodo learns, the Shire now no longer offers protection. The Wizard and the companions are at the door, the Road "that goes ever on and on / Down from the door where it began" (1:82) is before us, and the sun is rising. Like Frodo giving away all of Bag End and its belongings (even if to the Sackville-Bagginses, among others) we must, mentally or literally, cut our many links to the past, dispense with all that holds us back. Then we must, like Frodo at his first meeting with the Elves, question them (or whoever we meet as guides and wise companions) "much about happenings in the wide world outside the Shire" (1:92).

Then let us give a big party, literally or figuratively, for setting out is not only a solemn occasion, but also cause for a celebration. Leaving one world is to be born anew, born into a wider world of white-headed mountains, of Elves with the beauty of the stars in their faces, and of infinite sky.

It is the world not only of everyday duties, but of magic and legend. And as we enter, our new companions, visible and invisible, will say, "Hooray, a new child is born into *our* world."

The Theosophical classic *The Voice of the Silence* speaks of one who has well set out on the great journey, as though anticipating the Elven joys of Rivendell and Lothlórien, which are of a beauty and an encouragement only dreamed of in the Shire:

> Behold, O happy Pilgrim! The portal that faceth thee is high and wide, seems easy of access. The road that leads therethrough is straight and smooth and green. 'Tis like a sunny glade in the dark forest depths, a spot of earth mirrored from Amitabha's paradise. There, nightingales of hope and birds of radiant plumage sing perched in green bowers, chanting success to fearless Pilgrims.

Meditation — Leaving the Shire

Visualize or conceptualize around you all that is dear to you: persons, animals, places, objects of long and deep attachment.

Then place in this circle also those feelings, ideas, beliefs, concepts that are important to you.

Then see them begin to fade. Not because they are bad necessarily, but because they are not everlasting and the journey can commence without them.

Seeing them begin to fade is scary. Often we want to stop this process, or at least to save something, to pull something out. But to let them fade is the only way to begin the quest, like Frodo's selling his house. Yet those dearest to him, Sam, Merry, and Pippin, accompany him, not because he requires them to, or cannot let go of them, but because they come of their own free will, out of their love.

And we know that, like Bilbo and Frodo, after we have let go so we can leave on the quest, we will come back from the quest—and find anew what was left, but not as it was, not as necessary possessions, but as gifts to enjoy—for the secret is to be able to release in love, and then enjoy in love.

Now we must set out, whether the journey is an inward or outward pilgrimage.

And this particular quest, if it is the journey of the Ring-bearer, is not to find but to destroy. We are taking with us that which is the center of evil within ourselves and our world.

We know what it is: the thing in us that wants to dominate others or to make ourselves the center of the world, in overt or subtle ways. Take a moment to isolate this Ring of evil power—as it were to read the inscription on the Ring.

Through force, demand, argument, wheedling, charm, knowledge, status, with our money and our offices, in innumerable ways, we try to dominate others and bend them to our will in many areas of life. But all these means amount to the pathetic voice of a lack within ourselves that we want the other to complete. Or do we have additional ways of depending upon, ignoring, or undermining others? Do we try to drain from others the strength we lack, in the manner of a parasite to fill up what is wanting in our lives? All these are really the means of Mordor.

Instead, the way is love—letting others be who or what they were made to be in themselves, neither ruling nor draining—and letting our own love support their integrity, finding all we need within and then giving out of our own fullness. Love is giving out of the abundance in oneself; domination or draining is demanding because of the deficiencies in oneself.

Once the Ring of domination is destroyed, all else will be found easily, right at home. And the earth will rejoice in the freedom and abundance that arose spontaneously once the One Ring to rule them all is destroyed.

"Gandalf held it up. It looked to be made of pure and solid gold."
—chapter 2

3

Meeting the Guide

No one who has read and enjoyed *The Lord of the Rings* can forget Gandalf. His stooped frame, his aged but sharp-eyed face, his beard, staff, and smoke-wreathed pipe—all belong as much to Middle-earth as do Hobbits and the Shire. And in a real sense Gandalf is the pivotal figure in the story. He links past and present, the Shire and the world, and it is he who initiates and fosters the action.

When Gandalf tries directly to combat the power of Sauron, he is often surprisingly ineffective. Early in the story, he is tricked by Saruman, by then a collaborator with the evil force, into imprisonment at Isengard. For a long while, Gandalf and the Balrog are able to reach no more than a standoff, though finally that fell being comes to his ruin.

Gandalf works best through others whom he befriends and guides. He does not himself destroy the Ring, nor will he accept or carry it. He wisely realizes that its power joined with his own will corrupt him and in the end make him like the Dark Lord himself. When Frodo offers the Ring to Gandalf, the sage is for a moment tempted by its potential. For those of largeness of soul, the beginning of self-destruction often lies in thinking about the good one can do through the use of inordinate power. Indeed, Gandalf says that pity would be the soft spot through which the power of the Ring could enter into his heart—pity for all suffering creatures in the world and desire to alleviate their pain. But he knows it would not end there: "The wish to wield it would be too great for my strength" (1:71).

The bearing of the Ring and its destruction paradoxically will have to pass to one far weaker than himself, one innocent of the grand temptations that could parade themselves before a magus of Gandalf's spiritual magnitude. The Wizard shows excellent judgment in relying on Hobbits to care for the deadly circlet, though he comes more and more to understand its terrible and increasing dominion over first Bilbo and then Frodo. Later, when the hour comes for its destruction, he could not have done better than he does when he guides the tough-willed Bearer to undertake the perilous journey to the Cracks of Doom.

Like all true spiritual guides of humanity, Gandalf knows he can work only through others, whose freedom must be respected. In this he is like those adepts intermediary between this world and the divine in Ancient Wisdom traditions worldwide, including those called the "masters" in Theosophy. Some of the latter have even been identified as members of an inner "cabinet" guiding the world: Sanat Kumara, the "Eternal Youth" and "Lord of the World"; the Buddha; the Venetian; Serapis; Hilarion; the Master Jesus; Saint Germain, among others who include the conventional saints of several faiths, from St. Francis of Assisi to Kwan-yin.

Although this picture may strike some people as bizarre, it can be pointed out that nearly all great religious and Wisdom traditions offer an array of shining figures at the interface, so to speak, of transcendent divinity and the human level: angels and saints in Judaism, Christianity, and Islam; the buddhas and bodhisattvas of Buddhism; the deities and God-realized ones of Hinduism; the immortals of Taoism. These saints and holy ones have hidden but extensive powers to help and lead. Islamic mysticism speaks of "pivot saints" who may outwardly be only ordinary, unprepossessing people, yet whose inner work sustains the earth; should they fail, all would fall apart. Judaism has a similar tradition. What Theosophy does is merely make that pattern cross-cultural, as it were, recognizing such figures from many traditions. But whatever the names or ethnic traditions, the Ancient Wisdom insists there are those in or around this world in advance of the ordinary run of humanity who are able to serve as guides.

It is important to realize that in the Wisdom traditions, many of the adepts or saints are present in this world in physical bodies, like Gandalf. They may do their work of inner guidance from remote monasteries or hermitages, where they can be most undisturbed and free of unwholesome influences. But the great ones can also occasionally appear incognito walking the streets of a modern city, or even as a caller at one's apartment.

Wherever they may be, these elder brothers have control over little-known laws of nature, called "mayavic" powers, which enable them to work seeming miracles or magic, though strictly speaking the marvelous deeds are not that, but the exercise of sciences far beyond the common knowledge of the age. Thus adepts can assume various guises, be seen simultaneously at two places, and correspond through marvelously appearing "precipitated" letters. They can also communicate with their pupils through telepathy or dreams.

The Lord of the Rings, like Theosophy, tells us that such spiritually advanced individuals have mysterious roles in the guidance of humanity and all other beings on this planet. Individuals may become students or disciples of a particular guide, rather as Bilbo and Frodo are to Gandalf. It may be noted that the disciplic relationship is also salutary for the adepts, particularly if, as good masters should, they accept the relationship in humility and love, with a willingness to learn as well as to teach. Gandalf once tells Merry that all Wizards ought to have a Hobbit or two to take care of, to learn from that responsibility what "care" means and as a corrective to their pretensions (2:194).

The adepts' overall leadership of the world's development is indirect, like Gandalf's. Wizards or adepts may meet us at the growth parameters of our lives, guiding those of us open to growth through dreams, inner real-izations that seem to just "come," or seemingly accidental or coincidental occurrences. They may even visit us in some way at the right time in the guise of inexplicable "chance" meetings.

Yet real masters know they cannot force themselves on disciples, only help them freely choose for themselves the right course. They are no more than stimuli or catalysts, and they know that it is best for them to remain in the background. The Guardians are almost, in this respect, like forces of nature or the life-energy that surges through all living things—unseen, yet nourishers of that which is seen. Much that happens for good in the world would, if all were known, be seen as the result of impulses sent out from the adepts. But at our level of knowledge all is not known, and the guides prefer it so in this age of the world. As the Theosophist Henry Steel Olcott said of the masters' work in *Old Diary Leaves* (1:18):

> Unseen, unsuspected as the vivifying spiritual currents of the Akash, yet as indispensable for the spiritual welfare of mankind, their combined divine energy is maintained from age to age and forever refreshes the pilgrim of Earth, who struggles on toward the Divine Reality.

How then does Gandalf work as one of the world's guides in the Third Age? Refusing the power of a Ring-bearer, or even a ruler, he is first of all a caregiver: "But all worthy things that are in peril as the world now stands, those are my care" (3:30). As the full meaning of Bilbo's Ring dawns upon him, Gandalf comes to realize that the great task he has before him is the destruction of the Ring, and with that achievement his labors of caring will be fulfilled.

First, Gandalf is responsible for seeing that the Ring is recovered and entrusted to hands in which it will be as secure as possible—Bilbo's. This comes about through the Wizard's leading Bilbo almost by devious means to accompany the Dwarves on their quest to retrieve treasure from a drag-on. Clearly, at that time, Gandalf does not consciously know of the Ring's whereabouts—clutched by the pitiful Gollum at the roots of a mountain—or why Bilbo has to go with the Dwarves, or what the Hobbit will do in an episode that seems at the time a mere digression from that journey. Yet Gandalf says to Frodo concerning Bilbo's finding of the Ring, "Behind that there was something else at work, beyond any design of the Ring-maker. I can put it no plainer than by saying that Bilbo was *meant* to find the Ring, and *not* by its maker. In which case you also were *meant* to have it, and that may be an encouraging thought" (1:65).

At the time of the events that begin *The Hobbit*, Gandalf is only an unconscious or intuitive instrument for the Ring's destruc-tion. Yet his heart knowledge is well-honed. He often says, "My heart told me," and Gandalf remembers that, at the time that Bilbo found the Ring, a shadow passed over his heart, even though he did not then know its cause (1:57). Nonetheless, it is he who

Gollum

entices Bilbo into that journey through a combination of persuasion, intimidation, enchantment, and shame. And eventually he will know that he and Bilbo have played their parts because it was time for the Ring to pass to another for the ultimate defeat of Sauron and the ending of the Age.

Frodo comes to know Gandalf at first only casually, as a friend of Bilbo's who occasionally and usually unexpectedly drops in for a chat. When that period in the saga—between Bilbo's first adventure and his second departure—comes to a remarkable end with the long-expected party, Gandalf is again in evidence. Significantly, however, most Hobbits know him chiefly through his entertainment magic—the fireworks—and by a somewhat dubious reputation as one who led Bilbo, as he will later Bilbo's nephew Frodo, "off into the Blue" and away from whatever good Hobbit sense they may once have had.

There are contemporary Wizards and guides whose reputations in the world have not been dissimilar. According to Theosophical tradition, when the modern movement began in the nineteenth century, the masters commenced making their presence known first to selected individuals and then to many others through seemingly magical "phenomena." Later some of them wondered if the "phenomena" had not led to digressions from the real meaning of the Ancient Wisdom rather than to an understanding of it. The master called "K. H." began the early series of epistles later published as *The Mahatma Letters to A. P. Sinnett* with a refusal to convince the world of his powers through a public wonder (causing an edition of the London *Times* to appear in India on the day of its publication), as Sinnett had asked him to do. Gandalf, who is similarly aware of the danger of magic, also uses his greater powers only sparingly.

Next Gandalf employs another means, which is also used by the Theosophical adepts, namely the impartation of new knowledge about the world's secrets: its inner history, the locus of real peril and power in it today, and the nature of the quest now most needful. After long and puzzling absences following Bilbo's disappearance, the Wizard taps once again on

Frodo's study window. The two spend an evening and morning in which Frodo learns the wonderful and terrifying lore that lies behind the Ring, a story that takes them far back into the Elder Years. After Gandalf's final test of the ring's identity, the quavering Hobbit reads the dreadful fiery inscription on the ancient band he has received: "One Ring to bring them all and in the darkness bind them." And he begins to understand that his mission is the destruction of the Ring.

While that task unfolds, Gandalf employs yet another important device of the adept: he brings the principal disciple into contact with others of interrelated destiny, forming a network of companions in the quest. First the three Hobbits who are to accompany the Ring-bearer are brought together. In the Inn at Bree, they meet Strider, who eventually turns out to be far more than he seems at first. At Rivendell, the Ring party confers not only with Gandalf, who has been separated from them for a time, but also with Elves of deep memory and deeper wisdom in matters of the Rings, beginning with the Elf-ruler Elrond. The rest of the Nine Walkers who are to be the Ring's party are then added to the expedition. Legolas the Elf, Gimli the Dwarf, and Boromir the warrior from Gondor join Frodo, Sam, Merry, Pippin, Strider, and Gandalf.

During the talk at Rivendell, Gandalf, in telling his own story, reveals more of the roles of others caught in the web of the Ring. They speak of Sméagol or Gollum, the possessor of the Ring before Bilbo, his twisted mind still Ring-ridden. Gollum was captured by the Wood-elves and questioned by Gandalf, but Legolas reports that he has escaped. Although that is unwelcome news, Gandalf's enlightened intuition does not fail him; he comments about the pathetic creature, "But he may play a part yet that neither he nor Sauron have foreseen" (1:269).

Earlier, when Frodo wonders why Gandalf has let the captured Gollum live, saying angrily that he deserves death, the Wizard replies memorably. He acknowledges that Gollum probably deserves death, as do many that live. But then he adds that many who die deserve life, and asks if the Hobbit can give it to them. The silence that query evokes leads the seer to admonish Frodo not to be too hasty in pronouncing lethal judgments, for even the wise are not able to foresee all outcomes. His heart tells him, Gandalf adds, that the pitiful Gollum still has some role to play in the drama of the Ring, for he is bound up in its fate, past and future (1:69).

In addition to Gandalf, two other Wizards are named in the story: Radagast and Saruman. Radagast is clearly an adept of the wisdom of holy simplicity, whose path lies through the friendship of birds. Saruman is by now a magus of far more complex and devious character who has been corrupted by knowledge of and desire for the One Ring. He is able to use Radagast to trick Gandalf into visiting him at Isengard, where he will be held captive, though it is also one of Radagast's birds, the Great Eagle Gwaihir the Windlord, who rescues him.

When Gandalf the Grey comes to him, Saruman, who had once been known as Saruman the White, is robed in many colors. His visitor knows what that means. As Theosophy also tells us, even great masters and adepts can be enticed and brought over to the dark side. That, we are informed, is what has happened to Sauron himself, who seems once to have been one of the Eldar or High Elves. He was seduced by Morgoth, a fallen Valar who was the first source of evil in Middle-earth back in the First Age. Nothing, it is said, starts out evil, not even Sauron or his master (1:281).

It is possible to gain considerable inner power on the basis of skill only, without the great wisdom and compassion that is its true foundation. But according to the Wisdom teachings, those of such bent can never rise in the spiritual ascent above the mental plane, the highest level of separate individual thought, for evil magicians cannot see beyond the separate ego, or its gratification by power and the glittering products of power. Therefore they do not rise to the next level of consciousness, the buddhic, for it involves ego transcendence into cosmic consciousness and universal love—the realization of Oneness. In the Wisdom tradition, such turned beings are called "Brothers of the Shadow" or Ma-mo Chohans, equivalents

of the creative consciousnesses called Dhyan Chohans, but whose work is destruction on a large, even planetary, scale—and "who delight in personating gods and sometimes well known characters who have lived on earth" (*Mahatma Letters* 95).

Perhaps certain particularized outbreaks of large-scale evil, especially those that are utterly irrational and disproportionate to their cause, even for the often dismal annals of human history, may be the work of such evil Wizards of the Shadow and of Destruction, comparable to the Dark Lord of Mordor, whose hand has reached briefly into the stream of human affairs. Likely examples have not been lacking in twentieth and twenty-first century history. But of such matters we can only speculate, and too much such speculation is unwise.

Saruman

Gandalf, like Sauron, is always more than he seems. He is one of the five Istari, Wizards sent at the beginning of the Age to contest the power of Sauron and to bring together all those who resist him. They form an order, each member of which is identified by a color. Three are known: Saruman the White (later multicolored), Gandalf the Grey (later White), and Radagast the Brown. It is clear they are either Valar or Guardians themselves in human form, or closely related to them as "sons" or agents. They are sworn to the service of the "secret fire" of Anor, a word elsewhere referring to the Sun. But having come into Middle-earth, they have adopted frail, aging human forms and are neither all-knowing nor all-powerful, appearing much like the Druids or augurs of old.

Much the same can be said of the Theosophical adepts. In developed Theosophical lore, the head of our Solar System is the Solar Logos, whose outward manifestation is the Sun. The leaders of the hierarchy inwardly governing Earth are the Kumaras, Lords of the Flame, high envoys of the Solar Logos, sent to Earth some eighteen million years ago to oversee the evolution of beings like ourselves. The Kumaras are Sanat Kumara, the "Eternal Youth" and "Lord of the World," and three companions, who all dwell in Shambhala. The other masters of the invisible government may be of very highly evolved human extraction, but have reached a level of spiritual evolution permitting them to serve as subordinate colleagues of the Lord of the World, who is also called the "One Initiator," for he endows those ready for inner service with the active powers they will require.

Regardless of details, we see in both Middle-earth and the Wisdom tradition that at its apex the spiritual organization of our planet makes contact with unseen Guardians who have come from elsewhere, but who care about earth and, like all the truly great, are able to take on a humble vesture and role in order that they may work quietly from within for the welfare of the earth.

Nor are these masters all-knowing or all-perfect, as they are themselves careful to acknowledge. They are not gods. In the *Mahatma Letters* (450) the

Gandalf versus the Balrog

Master K. H. says, "We are not infallible, all-foreseeing 'Mahatmas' at every hour of the day," and elsewhere (39), "Being *human*, I have to rest." Gandalf also can get tired and make mistakes of judgment. He himself admits that he was at fault when he tells of being lulled by the words of Saruman (1:263). As we have seen, Saruman, once the leader of the Order of Istari, himself falls to a much worse state. Gandalf struggles for long hours at the gates of Moria, unable to get the magic formula to open its doors rightly. We have already noted his saying, very wisely, that even the wise do not know all ends.

Moreover, Gandalf is himself on the path of initiation, as are also the masters of other Wisdom traditions. At one point in the remote past, the Wizard of Middle-earth must have vowed service to the secret flame of Anor in some unimaginable rite. His battle with the Balrog deep in the earth, involving dark struggles in mysterious underground passages of which later he will not speak and resulting in his virtual death, can only be likened to an initiation, from which he emerges as a master of higher degree.

Thereafter he wears white and takes the place of Saruman as head of the Istari.

The ordeal of that lonely and dark battle is similar to what the Wisdom tradition calls the "fourth initiation," which brings the adept into consciousness of the buddhic plane and its indescribable joy and splendor of cosmic consciousness and universal love. It is this glory that evil magicians are denied, for they are unwilling to undergo that by which the separate ego-consciousness is transcended. As depicted by the Theosophical writer C. W. Leadbeater in *The Masters and the Path* (161), in the fourth initiation the candidate suffers abuse and then total abandonment:

> It is one of the features of the fourth Initiation that the man shall be left entirely alone. First he has to stand alone on the physical plane; all his friends turn against him through some misunderstanding; it all comes right afterwards but for the time the man is left with the feeling that all the world is against him.
>
> Perhaps that is not so great a trial, but there is another and inner side to it; for he has also to experience for a moment the condition called Avichi, which means "the waveless," that which is without vibration. The state of Avichi is not, as has been popularly supposed, some kind of hell, but is a condition in which the man stands absolutely alone in space, and feels cut off from all life, even from that of the Logos; and it is without doubt the most ghastly experience that it is possible for any human being to have.

This initiation has been compared to the crucifixion of Christ. In the case of Gandalf's solitary and titanic battle with the Balrog's dark energy, left over from a primordial age, one can well believe that for the Wizard it is a death and a rebirth. After the ordeal, he says, "Naked [like a newborn babe?] I was sent back—for a brief time, until my task is done" (2:106).

Gandalf's work in this world is a particular task, contesting the power of Sauron, and his time is the particular time in which that labor must be undertaken, the Third Age. He is well aware of this focus, saying, "All we have to decide is what to do with the time that is given us" (1:60). And again, noting that other evils may come after Sauron—for that minister of atrocity is himself now said to be only a servant or emissary—the Wizard adds, "Yet it is not our part to master all the tides of the world, but to do what is in us for the succor of those years wherein we are set, uprooting the evil in the fields that we know, so that those who live after may have clean earth to till. What weather they shall have is not ours to rule" (3:155). The Third Age is his age, and at its end his work is finished. The burden of the world thereafter lies upon those remaining behind, and upon the generations coming after them.

Comparably, the Theosophical masters do not abide forever in one rank or office, but just as they arrive at a particular role through initiations, so as they pass through higher and higher initiations, they may rise above the circles of this world altogether, like the company of the Ring sailing to the Undying Lands. It is suggested that they may then be able to undertake the work of a Solar Logos, or to work in a cosmic dimension beyond our imagining.

Application: Finding Our Wizard

Now let us think about our own lives in relation to the guides. How do we find our spiritual guide, our Wizard? There are several prospects.

First, it may be that the guide, or at any rate the quest to which you are being guided, may find you. This is certainly the case with Bilbo and

Frodo, who have to rise to the challenge of journeys with tasks they do not seek, and would certainly not have sought had they known what they would entail. Gandalf's and the Dwarves' request that Bilbo accompany them on the treasure hunt, in which he is to be their "burglar" in recovering the treasure from a dragon, comes to the Hobbit gentleman as an unwelcome surprise. Frodo, in turn, has no particular desire to inherit the Ring that the other Hobbit obtained on the earlier quest and even less to undertake its final destruction. These are simply tasks laid upon the Hobbits by God, providence, or fate, working through the Guardians, as they work through the guide "on the ground," Gandalf. The Hobbits' part is not finding the guide, but responding when he finds them, and they do that nobly in the end.

If you feel this prospect connects with the way your life works, then your place is not to go looking for a guide and a quest, but to remain acutely open to what comes to you. I have no doubt at all that guides and quests present themselves at some point—maybe at several points—in the lives of virtually everyone who reaches adulthood. But some opportunities may not even be seen because we are too busy staring in other directions. Many that are seen are dismissed because we are far too prone to say, "That's not for me," "That's too hard—I couldn't do it," "I don't have the right training," or "I have too much else to do." If we are really going to wait for the guide, and expect him to come—as he will if we truly wait with open eyes—we must be ready to go when he taps on our study window.

Second, one can of course make oneself very accessible to the guide by virtually making one's quest into a search for the guide. Helena Blavatsky, spiritual founder of modern Theosophy, spent the years roughly of her twenties and thirties traveling the world exploring mysterious phenomena, her passion for this quest eclipsing all else in her life. In the process, as she reported later, she eventually met her masters in the Himalayas. After much testing, she received the initiations that enabled her to keep in touch with them, as she embarked on her mature work of teaching and writing newly permitted arcana of the Ancient Wisdom for the modern world.

Her way cannot be recommended for most people. Most of us have other responsibilities to ourselves and those around us in our formative years. Preoccupation with one's personal spiritual quest to the exclusion of all else can, for most, become unbalanced and self-centered. Only a person with the very unusual calling of a Madame Blavatsky, for whom it was clear that this was all she could do and that her single-minded quest would lead in the end to unique world service, can rightly undertake it—and the cost to this exceptional woman was very, very high. But one can, if so led, do a good amount of lower-level spiritual exploration through reading and visiting various teachers and groups—now also through the use of tapes and videos—until one comes to the path one knows inwardly is right.

You will know it because you will respond to it without tension or mental reservation, because you feel respected and rightly guided by it but not manipulated or controlled, because it enhances who *you* really are at your best and highest, without trying to make you into someone else, and because you sense it leading to the true fruits of the spirit: love, joy, and peace.

Third, your guide may not be one single person. You may realize that too much dependence on one individual can be hazardous. The one-to-one relationship in spiritual guidance works well only with the wisest of guides and for the wisest of students. For the guide, the temptation of the Ring of Power—"I need to control these persons' lives because I know what is best for them"—can be strong. Likewise, the temptation for many pupils is to become too dependent, too used to having another make decisions for them even in such intimate matters as how to pray and meditate.

At best, a teacher-disciple relationship in this world ought to be short-term. It can be advantageous for a time, if the teacher is well-chosen, but bear in mind that every good teacher wants students to graduate. It is no credit to a teacher if students never seem to learn enough to be on their own. At the end of their quest, when Gandalf surprises the Hobbits by taking his leave as they are returning to the Shire, he tells them that his work is done and that they will have to take care of the Shire's problems themselves. That is, he adds, what they have been trained for, and he is quite confident they can handle the job. They have grown up and are ready to take their places as leaders rather than students (3:275). Don't trust teachers who cannot lay down their own burdens and say words like these.

Rather, if you follow this third way, learn from all whom you meet: the trash collector, the shop attendant, the mechanic, the co-worker, your spouse and children. All will say things at times that knowingly or unknowingly teach you something about the nature of God and the inner workings of the universe. Even your dog or cat may preach wordless sermons. Learn how to garner them by the method outlined in the meditation below.

And remember that people too can preach sermons without words. In the East, many great exemplars of the Way have been known as silent teachers. Truly enlightened teachers teach as much by the way they walk, the way they sit, the way they listen, the way they eat, and the way they work with their hands, as by what they say. In the true teacher, these acts say without tongue that all life is unified and all actions arise out of clear still depths within. As silently as the sun, such a person blesses all those around. One can receive powerful lessons in this way from good mechanics and from good gardeners.

Fourth, you may have an inner relation to a master. This is a way favored by many Theosophists, whose tradition supports the belief that one can learn from teachers not ordinarily visible, though they may be in physical bodies dwelling in a remote hermitage or may reside instead on one of the inner planes. Contact is maintained through dreams and telepathic impulses that bespeak new teachings, spark desire to follow new spiritual practices, or insist that one undertake a particular service. Judging from accounts in such classic Theosophical sources as Henry Steel Olcott's *Old Diary Leaves*, it is also possible for the adept, by mayavic power, to arrange unexpected encounters. One can never know whether that unusual person one meets, with whom one perhaps only exchanges a few words or per-haps has an interesting conversation, is one's teacher incognito or an agent of that teacher.

If you follow this path, take it seriously, not just as a pleasant fantasy. Realize that the connection of teacher and student is, as C. W. Leadbeater makes clear in his book *The Masters and the Path*, the result of long ded-ication to the preliminary virtues of the Path through study, meditation, service, and ethical living. It is, moreover, generally inaugurated by some definite sign of initiation, a dream or a very special unmistakable occurrence. After you feel the connection is made, maintain it by regular meditation in which you allow yourself to be open to messages from the teacher, and assess them in the way suggested below to try to make sure they are not merely from yourself.

Fifth, the master may be your own higher Self. This is certainly accept-able in principle, for the higher Self is the divine within, and has latent with-in it all the wisdom of God and the universe. The problem comes in finding the way to open the inner connection to this higher Self, so often blocked, in order that you can receive the influx of energy and ideas from it unim-peded. To seek the higher, spiritual, or Christ Self (as it has been variously called) as one's true guide is helpful but risky. The great benefit lies in the way that, again in principle, the guide is always present, but access to that guide requires great discernment and honesty.

It is easy to mistake for the divine voice any voice that speaks what *you* think God ought to say to you, or that you want God to say. The advan-tage of teachers outside yourself, even imperfect ones, is that they can give some sort of outside perspective, some corrective to your own attitudes. It is not only a matter of your inner voice saying smooth things you want to hear. Some people, overly convinced of their own unworthiness, are too harsh with themselves in what they think God would say to them, just as others are too gentle. Spiritual wisdom is always finding the true Middle Way, the point of equilibrium that is neither rigorous nor lax. If you follow your own higher Self as your spiritual guide, you are in the classroom of a teacher of teachers. But you need to be sure it is indeed that voice you are hearing, and not merely other students whispering to each other, or you talking to yourself.

How can we know which of these five methods of finding the master is authentic, or at least right for us, and which is not? The short answer is that we cannot, without very long experience and perhaps a few hard lessons. There is no sure litmus test. But ways can be tried.

The best test is still that of Jesus: By their fruits ye shall know them. Do this teacher and this path really lead to the good fruits of the Spirit: love, patience, growth, peace, and joy? Or do they lead instead to contention, anxiety, depression, and loneliness or regret? Does the teacher guide by loving speech and by the teacher's own life—for we can learn about a God of love only in a loving way—or is the guidance by bitter words? Does the teaching lead to a peaceful life or to anxiety over one's spiritual status? Is the path one of inner harmony and stability or of fluctuations of spiritual mood? Is the result of following the path community and contentment or isolation and longing for what one has given up?

Be very careful here. Of course a true spiritual path will have some hard parts, but even then, in some place very deep down in one's consciousness, one ought to know, like Frodo in Mordor, that this is the right way. And the true fruits of the Spirit ought also to be at least blossoming or budding all the way through.

Perhaps in the end the royal path is that of Bilbo and Frodo: allowing the guide subtly to arrange circumstances of life that present us with the challenges we need to face and, if we respond adequately, that set us on the quest we ought to follow. In the course of this discovery, the master may appear in person, like Gandalf, or through a representative. But like Gandalf, the master will not always be with you, or give you orders for every eventuality. You must then be on your own, able to receive guidance whenever and however it comes, even in a chance word from someone in the supermarket or, best, from your own inner teacher. But before you get such a message, you must pray for and receive the gift of discernment. And before that, you need to be in right relationship with the master.

If you follow the path of Bilbo and Frodo, here in review are the steps by which the inner or outer teacher-guides, in the manner of Gandalf to the Hobbits, may make themselves known:

• First minor "phenomena" or wizardy magic may occur around you, showing that something special is now breaking through: strange coincidences, inexplicable but significant signs, small "miracles."

• Then knowledge will be imparted to you even as it was to Frodo by means of Gandalf's conversation. But in your case it may be through guidance in finding the right books, tapes, lectures, or simply by implanting inner realizations of truth that come when needed. This special wisdom may begin with stories out of the remote past, but will come directly to the point of telling you who you *really* are, why you are here, and what you are supposed to do. Frodo receives teaching from Gandalf relevant to his mission step by step, first generally in "The Shadow of the Past" conversation, then more definitively when he accepts his awesome obligation at the Council of Elrond in Rivendell.

• At the same time, the guide will seem to arrange connections with others having particular relationships with that knowledge and that mission, like the Ring-bearer's new links to the other Hobbits, Strider unexpectedly encountered at Bree, and those fellow walkers he meets at Rivendell. You too will meet unexpected companions or supporters of your quest, who will come to you at the right time and place.

• Next the guide sees that you undergo certain initiations which, while hard, both wound and strengthen you, like Frodo's ordeal on Weathertop.

• Finally (and in a deep sense all the way through) the path you are on will produce the true fruits of the Spirit: a knowing that all this is really true growth, and a pervasive presence of love, joy, and peace in your life whatever outer storms there may be. When the heart is at peace, the discernment or heart-wisdom it needs will arise.

Meditation on Finding the Guide

Bring your consciousness to a one-pointed focus to stop the stream of thoughts jumping like a monkey from one thing to another: observe the breath going in and out, say a chant, steady the gaze on a single object like a candle flame or holy picture. By such means, still the mind until it is clear.

See within yourself the empty sky—calm, bright, and infinite. Let it remain still and clear for some time. Then allow billowing clouds to form.

Let the clouds open to reveal the face or symbol of your teacher.

Be still again for a long time.

Then hear the words the teacher speaks to you.

Just hear and receive them, without judging, evaluating, rejecting, or obeying them. Just listen with the inner ear.

After another time of stillness, get up. Hold those words in your mind, quietly, but think nothing more about them, neither approval nor disapproval.

Go about your work. If you were meant to have the message of those words now, they will have an effect on your thoughts, words, and deeds—on your attitudes and actions. They will have an effect of themselves.

Later think about what kind of fruits they brought forth in you that day. Did you feel more love, joy, and peace that day? Did any change feel like real growth, something really unfolding within you that was waiting to unfold, or did it feel like something that was "not me" stuck in from outside?

Then, when you hear other words that might be the voice of the master, from an encounter in the supermarket to the words spoken from a pulpit or at an ashram, receive them in the same way: hear, without willed judgment, rejection, or obedience. But hold those words quietly in your mind as you go about in the world. If the words affect your own thoughts, words, and deeds, let them do so, but do not force them to affect you.

Later think about what kind of fruits those words brought forth, and evaluate them accordingly.

Love. . .Joy. . .Peace.

Frodo and Boromir

4

The Weight of the Past

Behind the story of *The Lord of the Rings* hangs a golden cloud of names from far away and long ago: Elbereth, Númenor, the lost realm of Arnor. Such names are not just relics of the dead past. Much of the richness of the epic lies in the sense it evokes that heroic struggles in the present are only late chapters in immensely long stories tracing far back into the Elven mists of the Beginning and the First Age of the world. Swords flash and magic is muttered against the backdrop of a vast and ancient cosmos alive with powers both visible and invisible, some known and some only evocatively suggested in the lore of the Wise. When Éomer sees Hobbits, which he knows only from children's tales, he laughingly asks, "Do we walk in legends or on the green earth in the daylight?" Aragorn responds that we may do both. For the green earth under our feet is the stuff of legends past, and what we do on it now will make the legends of the future (2:37).

Legend is made real in the second chapter of *The Fellowship of the Ring*, "The Shadow of the Past." Reading it, we too may realize how little we truly understand the mysterious and immemorial influences on all levels of reality that have gone into the making of our lives and our times. The present day has been shaped by events large and small, seen and unseen; and if all were unveiled, we might see that causes seemingly small—donning a ring, a chance encounter between unimportant people—are the real creators of history. On the other hand, many events that loom large in the eyes of politicians, journalists, and conventional record-keepers may in fact be just flotsam and jetsam on the surface of deep and largely unknown currents. For the world may really be held together by those obscure pivot saints that Islamic mysticism speaks of, and wars may actually be started by the dark thoughts of those we too easily consider to be on humanity's margins.

What is written down in chronicles and histories is thus only the smaller part of what makes the world in which we must live. For we are sent into this world by our own mysterious, unfathomed

Aragorn

destinies, just as the universe itself seems to be held together far more by unseen "dark matter" than by light. The Ancient Wisdom always reminds us that the invisible history of the world is that of energies, battles, and drives for power and for peace on the inner planes, of which the outer is only the surface manifestation. Real history is the history of consciousness and its contents. C. G. Jung also addresses these matters in "The Meaning of Psychology for Modern Man" (148–9):

> When we look at human history, we see only what happens on the surface, and even this is distorted in the faded mirror of tradition. But what has really been happening eludes the inquiring eye of the historian, for the true historical event lies deeply buried, experienced by all and observed by none. It is the most private and subjective of psychic experiences. Wars, dynasties, social upheavals, conquests, and religions are but the superficial symptoms of a secret psychic attitude unknown even to the individual himself, and transmitted by no historian; perhaps the founders of religions give us the most information in this regard. The great events of world history are, at bottom, profoundly unimportant. In the last analysis, the essential thing is the life of the individual. This alone makes history, here alone do the great transformations first take place, and the whole future, the whole history of the world, ultimately springs as a gigantic summation from these hidden sources in individuals. In our most private and most subjective lives we arc not only the passive witnesses of our age, and its sufferers, but also its makers. We make our own epoch.

Other forces also help to plot the human story, from the point of view of both *The Lord of the Rings* and the Ancient Wisdom. Even the inner thoughts expressed outwardly by actors moving on the world stage reflect causes that are profounder still; psychic and subtle energies both within and around us cast quiet shadows on our minds. When Frodo awakes in the sanctum of the Barrow-wights, he feels nothing but the piercing cold fear of that ghostly place. Fear holds him and he dares not move, even though he is not restrained by a magic sword like the other three Hobbits.

What saves all of them is Frodo's remembering the song of Tom Bombadil. Its exuberant melody summons the presence of that jolly individual, and also evokes the joy, singing, and love for all that is green and fair which eddies around Tom so powerfully that his melody can overcome any contrary magic (1:152–4). Just as Tom's high spirits are the good cheer of the world's unstained beginning, so the fear Frodo feels represents a different sort of lingering weight of the past.

Barrow-wights, much like lost souls or rather earth-bound spirits, are able to possess the bodies of the dead—Frodo was able to cut off the hand of one such greenish, zombie-like corpse. But these earth-bound specters themselves are etheric or astral entities unable to let go of attachment to particular places or persons (appendix B). Even more powerfully, they are slaves to overwhelming desires: domineering loves, hatreds, fears, or addictions for drink or blood. Such "hungry ghosts" are "astral shells" left behind by departed souls, embodying only pitiful mindless fragments of what was once an individual, the higher centers having gone on beyond this world. The wights utter the empty, hollow sounds of miserable beings without the mind to know the cause of their misery—mutters and jumbles of hard and heartless words without logic or love (1:152).

The Barrow-wights prepare us to understand the Nazgûl, the Ring-wraiths or Black Riders, for the latter present the same phenomenon at a far more ominous level of development, thanks to their sharing in Sauron's power. The wraiths' facelessness to ordinary eyes—and even more their motivation by hatred and their essential weapon, fear—proclaim their character. They are lower astral beings defined by their hatreds, which are those of the Dark Lord. Such astral beings project around them the world in which they live, a world that reflects their attachments and desires, in this case cold dread and hatred.

The Nazgûl's master, Sauron, is the Dark Lord of the lower astral realm—a world by which he himself is enslaved and blinded. Gandalf says

A Nazgûl

of that Enemy: "But the only measure that he knows is desire, desire for power; and so he judges all hearts." In this, the Wizard adds, lies the Ring-bearer's best hope, for it would not occur to the Dark Lord that any being could possess the Ring and not want to use it to gain all power for himself. In the shadow of this Sauronic illusion, Frodo—seeking only to destroy the tiny concentrate of malevolent force—can creep toward the Cracks of Doom while the Enemy looks elsewhere expecting the rise of a rival (1:282).

The Nazgûls' high visibility only under the black light of the Ring proclaims their astral nature, for the Ring transfers its wearers into the lower astral realm, where they are invisible on the material plane but see quite distinctly the denizens of that grim world. Above all—increasingly even when not wearing it—the Ring-bearer shares in the fundamental dynamics of the lower desire plane. The turbulent life of that plane is driven, not by the healthy emotions and material things of this world, but by raw craving in its primal form—by hate, fear, and empty desire for what it can no longer have but is unable to transcend. The movie version of *The Lord of the Rings* provides a vivid and terrifying vision of the lower astral realm whenever Frodo puts on the Ring.

A second, more positive, way in which the weight of the past reaches into our own times is through the power of story to remind us of forces older and greater than even those of astral hate and fear. Providential powers, which are no less rooted in the far past than malign ones, are still active in present events: Gandalf telling Frodo that Bilbo was meant to find the Ring, and *not* by its maker. It is only the oldest and deepest stories that can convey such meaning as this, and they are the most hopeful.

The background stories in *The Lord of the Rings* are like the great myths of all peoples, and were intended to be so. Significantly, we find that whenever particular peril arises, the old legends are named. Gandalf tells the tale of the Ring to Frodo as the crisis begins, and tells it economically, saying that all Frodo needs to know is how the Ring had come to him as his responsibility. Yet at the same time the Wizard refers to the time in the distant past when the men of Westernesse came to the aid of Elves in resisting the Enemy: "This is a chapter of ancient history which it might be good to recall; for there was sorrow then too, and gathering dark, but great valour, and great deeds that were not wholly vain" (1:61). Stories out of the far past can hearten us in our struggles today.

On Weathertop, as the company begins to feel the fearsome power of the Ringwraiths, Sam asks to hear a tale of the elder years, "a tale about the Elves before the fading time." He wants to hear about Elves, he says, especially as the dark moves in close around the lonely party (1:203).

While Sam and Frodo are in the horrible desolation of Cirith Ungol, keeping up their morale by thinking of old stories of Beren and the Silmaril, Sam acutely observes that in the phial of light that the Lady Galadriel gave Frodo, there is a living link to the days of golden legends. "Why, to think of it," he exclaims, "we're in the same tale still! Don't the great tales never end?"

Frodo replies that, while the tales never end, the people in them come and go, and Sam then realizes that they themselves, there in the heart of darkness, are the living actors in a tale that in some future time people will tell around the fireplace or read out of a great book with red and black letters, even as they are recalling stories from out of what to them is the past. The story itself goes on forever, though with new settings and new heroes in each age and generation (2:320–1).

Sam Gamgee

When Frodo and Sam are with Faramir and his men in their cave to the east of the Great River, a tiny band in the midst of the Enemy, the Hobbits note that before they eat, their hosts turn and face west for a moment of silence. "So we always do," said Faramir, "we look toward Númenor that was, and beyond to Elvenhome that is, and to that which is beyond Elvenhome and will ever be." Frodo, admitting he has no such custom, feels "strangely rustic and untutored" (2:284–5).

Myth and story, or even allusions to the tales we know, shape our functioning view of the world and give us strength by putting the present moment, dark as it may be, into the foreground of a richly-colored painting with deep perspective. A myth expresses the worldview of its people in narrative form, showing how symbols and ways of living come to be. In *The Lord of the Rings*, stories about the first Elves, Dwarves, men, Hobbits, and Ents are told or sung with wistful yearning for the glory of the sunrise times of the Beginning, and call up renewed solidarity with those heroes and all their kindred. Great myths not only tell a story, they also reveal the essential character and subjective mood of the folk they speak about. We learn in the old songs and stories of the Elves' starry-hearted gladness and mysterious sorrows, of the Dwarves' tenacity and quickness to anger, and of human beings in their heroism and pride.

Myths or stories reveal not only facts or pseudo-facts, but more importantly feelings and images called archetypes. These powerful mental pictures tell more than any words can, though they may be evoked by words. In the stories of the distant origin of Middle-earth, in the time when the first Elf-children of the elder kindred opened their eyes to the beauty of land, sea, and stars, we see that, at its beginning, all beneath the sky was shot through with joy and light. Tom Bombadil, the eldest of all, remembers Middle-earth when it was entirely fair and one could walk fearless at night under the stars.

These stories remind us that despite the presence of the Dark Lord and the Land of Shadow, Middle-earth still retains glory whenever the stars can be seen or whenever the sun shines on leaves and ponds. For Middle-earth is shaped not only out of its own material nature, but by the Valar or Guardians. Myths of origin tell us about the real, final nature of things, for we humans tend to think that if we understand where something comes from, we know about its inmost nature and meaning. In that case, the ultimate reality in both Middle-earth and the Undying Lands is beauty and consciousness.

The most important of all Theosophical texts is H. P. Blavatsky's major work, *The Secret Doctrine*, an extended commentary on the "Stanzas of Dzyan," relatively short poetic fragments that express in ancient and enigmatic words a story of the origin of the world. Most of the book is an exposition of the Stanzas' meaning, relating to the early ages and primordial humanity. The first Stanzas tell a story like that of the Valar, for they say:

> The eternal parent wrapped in her ever-invisible robes had slumbered once again for seven eternities.
>
> Time was not, for it lay asleep in the infinite bosom of duration.
>
> Universal mind was not, for there were no Ah-hi [the Dhyan Chohans, similar to the Valar] to contain it. . . . The seven sons were not yet born from the web of light.

But then a solitary ray of light awakens life within the Mother, the Seven are aroused, and the universe is made, as "a web whose upper end is fastened to spirit—the light of the one darkness—and the lower one to its shadowy end, matter."

Chapter Four

This world is fundamentally good, yet ill has come into it—a world full of light yet not without shadow. Tolkien's stories tell us that the Dark's beginning in the Elder Days was the rebellion of Melchar, one of the Valar. He was tempted by the three Silmarils, which the High Elves created as jewelry of such beauty that none can see them and remain unmoved. Melchar is known in Middle-earth as Morgoth, and Sauron was originally his servant.

This story depicts evil stemming from an act of will. Melchar presumably knew the consequences of rebellion against the One and the other Valar, but he chose nonetheless to use the freedom of choice possessed by all knowing beings. All are free, for among them oneness is a matter not of force but of love, which can only be freely given. But Melchar, like Milton's Satan, preferred to reign in hell than be a slave (as he saw it) in heaven, and proceeded to make hells in what had been the beauty of Middle-earth.

It is sometimes said that Western and Eastern religions differ in that Judaism, Christianity, and Islam believe the main source of evil to be prideful rebellion against God, whereas Hinduism and Buddhism believe it to be ignorance, *avidya*, not seeing things as they really are. According to the concept of *avidya*, in our stupidity we mistake our ever-changing selves and petty desires for reality, while overlooking true reality, the oneness of all things.

Between the two, *The Lord of the Rings* is clearly on the Western side. But the twain may not really be in polar opposition to each other. Rebelling against absolute divine Reality surely starts from what can only be called "willful ignorance," for anyone with eyes open should see how futile and pointless that attack is. On the other hand, the ignorance of one who refuses to recognize the true nature of things, despite all evidence and all teaching, must be perverse and in some way insurgent against the light.

Evil as rebellion suits the dramatic needs of a novel, whereas evil as ignorance answers certain philosophical considerations. But the actuality is more complex than either view alone. The Ancient Wisdom recognizes several sources of evil, because to reduce suffering to just one cause makes it more rational than it is. Evil is nothing if not the irrational, that which ought not to be, yet is—"the abomination of desolation standing where it ought not," in the expression of Jesus; the "mystery of iniquity," in the term of St. Paul. Among Theosophical interpretations of the mystery of iniquity are the duality and multiplicity built into the manifest universe, karmic cause and effect, evolution, the necessity of an ordeal if we are to be initiated, and the activity of evil magicians in particular times and places.

Whether we are aware of it or not, we are voyagers on pilgrimage across the seas of space and time, gradually riding with the tides back through storm and sun to the Halls of Light, our true home, whence we came. But like mariners tacking about on that long crossing, in the anxiety of our separateness we think more of personal action and response than we contemplate oneness. When the self-centered impulse reaches the level of the evil Wizard's fear, hatred, and power, it amounts to rebellion against the One, and in the dark waters we see the wake of Satan or Sauron. More often, one hopes, we manage to keep the distant polar constellations to starboard as we bear toward the Uttermost West.

How can we find stories that bring the weight of the past to bear positively in our own lives?

First we need to realize that the point of such stories is *not* to translate them from story to allegorical abstractions, to say that Sauron "really" means abstract evil, Frodo some abstract ideal of courage, and so forth. This is the kind of allegory that Tolkien rightly disliked. Abstractions, though they may provide tools for universal application (the term Tolkien preferred), are not truer than story. Indeed, they may well be deceptive, seeming to represent some truth profounder than the naive-sounding surface meaning of a myth, whereas they are actually nothing but noise compared to the real music of human life.

Our *lives* are not abstractions, but stories. Story can therefore really tell human truths better than abstract words. The idea is not to find bloodless phrases to sum up the complex meaning of a human life, but to find the right way to tell its story. This is why the abstractions of philosophy, psychology, and science can never supersede myths, stories, novels, and epics as instruments for getting at the heart of our lives and dilemmas and their ultimate meanings.

Some of us have too easily acquiesced in saying that the abstractions of science and philosophy are "truer" than the stories of myth and religion. While the former have their place, what they really do, if taken as final, is break the link between our own story and the story of the universe. In the word picture drawn by those abstractions, we are conscious but the universe is not. Scientific abstractions, whether of physics, biology, or psychology, see only the material surface, that which can be weighed and measured, and philosophical abstractions too easily reduce life to words. If we didn't know better, science and philosophy would tell us that we ourselves are only what can be weighed and measured, or that we are only abstractions like "Life" or "Mind." We know we are something more, but it is hard for us to believe the rest of the universe is also something more, since we see only its lifeless surfaces.

The loss of the link between our own stories and the world story has left us in the wasteland of modernity. The yearning void opened by this disconnect helps to explain the continued power of religions that preserve the link, even if sometimes in naive form, as well as the popularity of Tolkien's world, where story is still strong.

It is important that the inward avenue between personal nature and universal nature be kept open. The nature of that road may be as mysterious as the way to Lothlórien, but its reality cannot be denied. For we are children of the universe. We came out of it. Whatever our nature—consciousness included—may be, it must somehow be "out there" as well, at least potentially, and our origin and destiny is the universe's origin and destiny as well.

Whether the Book of Genesis, the Stanzas of Dzyan, or *The Lord of the Rings* are "literally" true is not as important as how we feel and think about ourselves when we read them. Do they open for us that sense of the infinite mystery in life and consciousness that no abstraction can ever quite accommodate? Do they make us feel that, whatever the appearances and whatever the words, we have personal sources deep in the enigmas of space and time and a destiny wonderful beyond imagining? Do they give lightness and joy to the living of our present days, whatever happens?

Ask yourself, then, what the important stories in your life are. Not just the religious or historical stories you were taught, but the stories from whatever source that are *really* important, that arise of themselves in your mind when you need to know who you are, how you should act, what you want to be like. What mythical or personal story do you tell yourself in times of crisis and peril?

The story you turn to may be one that was told to you in childhood, possibly one important in your family, ethnic group, or spiritual community. There are people who draw powerfully from the courage of the Christian martyrs, the strength of African Americans under centuries of slavery, the self-sacrificing love of Jesus, or the great peace of the Buddha. Many Jewish families remember forebears who bravely immigrated to a strange new land, often with little more than hope in their pockets and often to escape terrible pogroms in the old country. You may have heard stories like these from your parents or in school or church or temple.

Or the stories that *really* affect you may not be from any communal or "official" lore, but from a novel or the movies. You are "really" like, or want to be like, Dorothy of Oz or Luke Skywalker of *Star Wars*, and sometimes you imagine yourself in her ruby slippers, or as him in his stifling setting but dreaming of the space academy. Sometimes such stories can be almost subversive: a generation identified with Holden Caulfield in *The Catcher in the Rye* despite, or because of, his many imperfections. You have to start where you are.

On the other hand, stories can be literally one's own: memories that somehow seem significant in telling who you really are, what your true values are, and how you are supposed to live your life. Some important recollections are from childhood: a family holiday or your first puppy or kitten. Most people remember their first day in school, first trip to a foreign country, first falling in love, and first day on an important job. And you remember typical days too, of childhood, marriage, or work, that show how you spend your ordinary times. Sometimes it is remembrance of ordinary life that most sustains one in extraordinary crisis. Frodo, in finding the courage to leave the Shire on his great quest, says that as long as he knows the snug and secure Shire is still there, he can endure the wandering, even though he might not himself see its gently rolling green fields and softly lit villages again (1:71).

Whatever your stories are, they are close to your basic identity and the part you are meant to play in the vast drama of the universe. Reflect on them for a moment. What do these personal narratives really say about you? Are the several stories that are really important to you—from family, school, religion, movies, novels, or personal memory—consistent in the picture they give of you and the values they present? If not, is this something you should think about?

Let's be honest. We are not necessarily exactly the same person at all times, but may use somewhat different values and self-images, and therefore different stories, in various situations: work, family life, recreational sports, trips away from home. How well do these fit together? Is any one image the *real* me and the others just roles I can put on? In a complex civilization like ours, such issues are complex. Adaptability to different situations, as well as radical consistency, can be a virtue, even an expression of compassionate love. But it never hurts to be fully aware of how one is living. Ask yourself, "How much do I like the way I am living? Are there changes to be made?"

The important question is, "Whatever the stories on which I base my life, does each represent the best I can be in its situation?" The "best" may not be the most effective in worldly terms, but instead the best way of expressing the higher divine self in a particular setting. The way we play amateur softball may not be the same way we sell insurance or parent a child, but the story that goes with each life role ought to show the best way to share love, joy, and oneness in that time and place. The stories behind you should make divine life happen on the level of your life. So get the best stories you can.

Meditation on Stories and the Past

Sit quietly in a reflective mood.

If someone were to ask you what story from past or present lore best expresses your life, best tells your story, what would it be?

It doesn't matter where it came from: family, faith, cinema, book, or memory.

Don't try to figure out the answer logically. Just take the first story that comes to mind.

Hold it in your mind for a moment, making sure you have the story clear and vivid.

Walk yourself through it from beginning to end. Identify with every part, experience every feeling, and bring the narrative to a successful or meaningful outcome.

Then sit quietly in a reflective mood again. Let the experience of that story sink deeply into your life.

Later think back on that story. Ask yourself if it is really the one you want to have and if it represents the best you can be. It may be a story for your past, but not for your present or future. Or perhaps it is for you now, but only needs to be understood and lived more deeply.

Whatever the outcome, be happy with your story. Know that it is you and that you are loved and blessed by the powers of the beginning and the end of that story, and by all Beginnings and Ends.

Pippin

5

The First Initiations

The four Hobbits destined to become Companions of the Ring—Frodo, Sam, Merry, and Pippin—leave the Shire and enter the strange Old Forest on September 26. The first great segment of their journey lies between the Shire boundaries and Rivendell, the Elven hall; on the way they are joined by Strider in Bree. At Rivendell, the Last Homely House, they meet Gandalf once more, as well as Bilbo and the Elf-ruler Elrond; and there the remaining four of the Nine Walkers—Gimli, Legolas, Boromir, and Gandalf himself—join the company.

During this initial part of the adventure, between the Shire and Rivendell, three episodes occur that amount to initiations for the Hobbits. Each entails an experience of virtual death, and a remarkable victory over that death. From our perspective, each victory brings a vision of the esoteric meaning of one or more of the planes of reality as understood by Theosophy, each plane further in and nearer to the divine self than the one before. (Appendix B gives a summary description of the planes.)

The first initiation happens in the Old Forest, when Merry and Pippin, caught and nearly killed by Old Man Willow, are saved by Tom Bombadil.

That remarkable being and his beloved wife Goldberry, more than any other beings, are fully at home with the physical and etheric planes and with their powers.

The second initiation is on Weathertop, where Frodo is attacked by the Ringwraiths. They give him a baleful vision of the lower astral plane, which is the Ring's true home and the realm to which all fascinated by its power are drawn.

The third initiation is at the Ford of Bruinen, where the party is nearly defeated again by the wraiths, but is rescued by Glorfindel and Gandalf. Those two high beings bring the Walkers to the haven of Rivendell, with its joyous and exalted air reminiscent of the mental plane.

The First Initiation: Physical

Why does the experience in the Old Forest suggest initiation into the profound depths of physical and etheric life? Recall Frodo at his wit's end running down a path faintly crying *help! help! help!* as his two companions are being squeezed to death by the heartless, ancient tree called Old Man Willow. Then a "deep glad voice" singing nonsense resounds carelessly and happily, "Hey dol! merry dol! ring a dong dillo!" and next "Goldberry, Goldberry, merry yellow berry-o! Poor old Willow-man, you tuck your roots away!" To their amazement the harassed travelers see a short little man with great yellow boots on his thick legs. He has a blue coat, long brown beard, bright blue eyes and a face "red as a ripe apple, but creased into a hundred wrinkles of laughter" (1:130–1). To their even greater amazement, the tree obeys him.

He is Tom Bombadil, and he takes the four distraught Hobbits down a merry trail, over a stone threshold, and into his rustic house with its dark polished wood table and many candles. By that board stands his spouse,

Goldberry, River-daughter, with her long yellow hair and gown green as young reeds. For two nights and a day the party enjoy the hospitality of Tom and Goldberry, learning much from the talk of their host. Tom tells the wanderers of the inner meaning of the forest, of the ways of trees and strange creatures, "cruel things and kind things, and secrets hidden under brambles." And, "as they listened, they began to understand the lives of the Forest, apart from themselves, indeed to feel themselves as the strangers where all other things were at home"— always a salutary lesson for humans (1:141). Tom tells his guests as much as they can grasp of his mysterious role as knower of these things, and the first secret was that he is Eldest. Tom tells them about the worlds before rain or river, before seed or tree, and he recalls the day those wonders first appeared under the sky of Middle-earth. He saw the seas rise, and the Elves troop

Tom Bombadil

westward. He knew eventides when one could walk fearless under the stars, and he felt the night darken when the Dark Lord came (1:142).

Tom suggests primal unfallen humanity in Eden or perhaps in the "Imperishable Sacred Land" of Theosophical tradition, the first home of the earliest human beings. He lives in harmony with nature in a wonderful way almost incomprehensible to us. On the profoundest level one can imagine, he intuits the inner life and feeling of nature and all its myriad beings, and he calls all its creatures by their names, like Adam naming the animals. He is able to name all creatures correctly because he understands each as a being in its own right, having a life of its own apart from that which humans impute to it and in a natural home to which humans are strangers. Tom Bombadil incarnates material, physical, embodied life in the fullest manner possible. Living out of its rich, joyous energy, he goes harmlessly and powerfully singing through the world of wild things, knowing what lies behind the eyes or leaves of each.

Goldberry

It also clearly goes without saying (for Tolkien, a Victorian at heart, such matters always went without saying) that Tom's relation to Goldberry is fully and gladly physical, characterized by an innocent sexual vitality continuous with the delighted love songs that he, after all the ages of the world, never tires of singing to her and that kindle light in the eyes of both when they come together in their hall of love and laughter. They must have completed their love in that nest, so out of the way of the larger world that it seems to be in the only human clearing among forests, mountains, and rivers without end—a cathedral for nature set amid the endlessly varied life of the wilds.

In all Tom's and Goldberry's physical joy, and in ours when fully realized, the etheric plane shimmers over the physical, sparkling like the twinkles in their eyes. Etheric matter or energy is a sort of mold for the physical body, and also represents the energy field around a living being. It is perceptible to the eye of science in what is called Kirlian photography, beautiful auras of color and dynamic form comprised of electric energy around flower and finger, as well as visible by extrasensory perception. The etheric "body" and its plane are likewise involved with the energy called "prana" by Indian Yogis, and "qi" or "chi" ("ki" in Japanese) by the Chinese Taoist adepts and martial artists of East Asia. It amounts to what is called the "Force" in the *Star Wars* movies.

This energy is sent by yoga practitioners to different parts of the body for healing, and can, according to stories, be employed by an adept to light a fire across a room or knock down an opponent without physical touch. We can think of it as a field of vital energy potentially embodying the exalted joy one feels not only *in* Tom Bombadil, but all around him as it flows from that singular creature to the atmosphere he breathes. The etheric force is alive and sparkling with rainbow colors as it rushes delightedly between Tom and Goldberry. That primal pair would not have been what they are without the full engagement of their etheric as well as their physical bodies.

How about us? Our existence in a physical body is evident. But the question is, how well do we live in our physical bodies? Do we live physically with the freedom and grace of Tom Bombadil, or do we slide into the lethargy and paralysis of fear that comes over the Hobbits in the Old Forest? Do we need physical-body initiations?

Tom's lightness and energy contrast with the tension and rigidity we often sense in our own bodies. Wilhelm Reich, a controversial psychoanalyst, spoke of the "body armor" we don as we stiffen and shrink physically in response to long-ago traumas or fears. We sit tense and rigidly upright in certain social situations, harden at the physical touch of another, or cringe at the sight of a dog like one that bit us. To relax the tension, we may turn to such addictive drugs as tobacco or alcohol.

Here we can speak only briefly and generally of initiations that liberate the body from its armor. The answer is not hedonistic indulgence of the flesh, for the flesh is not meant to be an end in itself, but rather a vehicle of the higher planes (etheric, astral, mental, and others), which function through it. The body will never be satisfied by mere hedonistic pleasure, for it is not intended to be the recipient of pleasure for its own sake, as though it were just a pampered and dissolute child.

As a vehicle, the body is instead an honest workman with a job to do. Like any workman, it deserves a fair wage, reasonable hours, good health, and a decent home. But also like any good workman, it really wants to do its work, and becomes restless and deeply dissatisfied with nothing but leisure and indulgence without challenge. Actually, what we call the lusts of the flesh—inordinate desire for exotic or inappropriate food, drink, drugs, or sex, in forms not necessary and often deleterious to sound physical health—do not come from the honest workman but are provoked by mirage images out of the lower astral plane, the realm of distorted desire.

To let the body be itself as a vehicle, we must let it be itself as sheer energy and joy. Let it work, exercise, play, dance, enjoy married and family intimacy, or sit quietly contemplating the beauty of nature, art, or home. Even let it be sick and know without rancor the sensations, the pure experience, of illness or pain. For all is good in its beginning and is so at its deepest roots. Let all you do in the body be done with the grace and inner delight of one who, like Tom, is truly free *in* the body: free from armor, free from astral phantasmagoria, free from wanting to be free of the body. Be yourself free *in* the fleshly vehicle, whatever its age or appearance, whatever its limitations—for any body that lives can ripple with some degree of delight in its life.

To live freely requires initiatory experiences that put you thoroughly in touch with all of your body. Yoga, body scanning, martial arts, self-aware sports (see books with titles like *Zen Golf* or *The Inner Game of Tennis*), or just doing it your own way—digging, working, hiking—are all paths through initiatory ordeals into the temple of the body. For they, like all physical activity, begin with effort, may very well pass through bodily pain, and then finally rise into the ecstasy known to athletes as "runner's high" or being "in the zone."

In all this doing, don't forget the etheric plane around the physical and intermixed with it. Keep it alive, along with your purely physical nature, through awareness not only of what the body is doing, but of the life, the vitality, the tingling electricity of its active flesh. When you contact others in the zone of that power, transmit it to them and be sure they feel it too. To share on the etheric plane, so that the subtle energy field of one person is perfectly harmonized with that of another, is perhaps the highest fulfillment of the physical and etheric planes. Be initiated into this joy, like Tom and Goldberry.

One curious thing about Tom: although he is shown the Ring by Frodo, it has no power over him and he can barely understand what it means or what to do with it. He even put it on—and did not disappear! Later, at the Council of Elrond in Rivendell, when the possibility of giving the Ring to Tom for safekeeping is raised, Gandalf replies that Bombadil might take it if all the free folk of the world begged him, "but he would not understand the need. And if he were given the Ring, he would soon forget it, or most likely throw it away. Such things have no hold on his mind" (1:279).

Tom's unconcern with the Ring is due to the fact that the Ring belongs essentially to the astral plane, and Tom's world is not astral but the fullness of the physical and etheric—a fullness so complete that it embraces levels of vision and vitality that for him are complete and all-absorbing in their wholesome physical and etheric nature. Therefore astral desire-formed realities, including the Ring, have no hold on him, as though they are construed in a language he does not speak. But for us, as for Frodo burdened with the Ring, the astral plane is indeed real, sometimes all too real. It is this plane that is manifested in the Hobbits' second initiation.

The Second Initiation: Astral

First let us review the story. On the slopes of Weathertop mountain, as night falls, black figures, blacker even than the surrounding gloom, come near. The dim shapes and the Hobbits' own strange deeply uneasy feelings tell those travelers and Strider that spectral adversaries are silently approaching. The Black Riders (also called Ringwraiths or Nazgûl) stalking the companions are themselves faceless; one can see only their black garb, which, as Gandalf later says, "they wear to give shape to their nothingness" (1:234).

Strider speaks to the Hobbits about those wraiths in ominous words that make clear their astral nature: "They themselves do not see the world of light as we do, but our shapes cast shadows in their minds, which only the noon sun destroys; and in the dark they perceive many signs and forms that are hidden from us. . . . Senses, too, there are other than sight or smell. We can feel their presence—it troubled our hearts, as soon as we came here, and before we saw them; they feel ours more keenly. Also . . . the Ring draws them" (1:202).

The Ring is highly activated by the presence of the servants of its dread maker. As they press in, Frodo finds the desire to put on the Ring more and more irresistible. Finally he can restrain himself no longer, and when the terrible circlet is on his finger, he suddenly sees the physical world only as if in a gray fog, but the shapes become horribly distinct. He perceives the five tall personages, seeing plainly the "keen and merciless eyes" in their white faces, their silver helms and steel swords, and on one a crown. Gandalf subsequently tells Frodo, "You were in gravest peril while you wore the Ring, for then you were half in the wraith-world yourself, and they might have seized you. You could see them, and they could see you" (1:234).

As they attack him, Frodo manages to cut the black robe of one of the Ringwraiths with his own blade, but when the wraith's icy blade pierces his shoulder, he falls to the ground crying, *O Elbereth! Gilthoniel!*—names of the Elven star-queen of yore. Then with a last effort before fainting, Frodo slips off the Ring.

Strider manages to repel the enemies with blazing brands of wood, for they dislike fire, and no doubt also because they believe the fragment of the cold magical dagger they have left in the Hobbit's flesh will work its way to his heart and bring him, and the Ring, into their wraith world without further effort on their part. Indeed, despite the healing arts of Strider, the Ring-bearer is very sick; he is given to falling often into a daze in which the outer world seems to fade. The events at the Ford of Bruinen, when the party is barely saved from the Nine Ringwraiths by the power of Gandalf and the Elves of Rivendell, he sees only in a haze.

Later, after the knife splinter has been removed by Elrond and the Hobbit is recovering, Gandalf tells him that he was starting to "fade" as the wound's power grew over his whole being, and in only a few more hours he would have been lost to the world of light (1:231). Frodo, in other words, was hovering between the physical-etheric and astral planes, with all the desire force of the wraiths bent to pull him over to their lower astral realm, the true home of the Ring. It was, as Gandalf says, touch and go. The Wizard is also aware that Hobbits can have unexpected reserves of strength, and though Frodo faltered seriously by putting on the Ring, his last remaining ounce of energy was enough to save him. But as Strider says, it was not so much Frodo's puny sword as the name of Elbereth that caused the deadly king to withdraw (1:210).

The astral field, from references to it so far, must seem negative: the realm of the Ring, the Ringwraiths, the Barrow-wights. Yet that is not the whole story. As the Desire realm, it is simply the universe as it would be constructed by the wants and attachments of each individual in it. This realm is therefore in all of us, continuous with our wanting and feeling faculties, and—like our desires—it expresses itself on many levels. It is our angry, fearful, craving self, and also much of our dreaming self, and finally our creative self in areas from homemaking to high art, in so far as these are noble and refined reflections of the self and its yearnings. Thus the astral realm encompasses the whole range of human desire, from the basest perverted lusts of the sadist, through normal human aspirations for family and comfort, to the lofty passion of the artist and poet for immortal beauty.

The astral plane is the first home of most of us after death, when we drop both the dense physical body and the etheric body to live in the astral or desire realm until our impulses on its level have worked themselves out. It may be that during our astral postmortem life we rise from lower to higher levels of that plane, as the lower desires are progressively exhausted and dropped, leaving only more and more exalted ones. Finally, when beauty and all that is good can be appreciated in a wholly nonattached way, the need to abide in the desire realm is completely transcended.

Initiation into and through the astral plane, like any initiation, must involve ordeal. It must begin at the bottom with fear and suffering. What this means is that we must face and comprehend our inner astral-plane side, beginning at its lowest level. But we do not have to enter it on its own terms, as Frodo did by succumbing to the temptation to don the Ring, nor should we.

Though there are magical, as well as plain fantasy, ways of entering the world of lower astral beings or summoning them up, those beings are to be avoided at all costs, unless one is a highly evolved adept able to meet them strictly for the purpose of helping those debased but pathetic wraiths. For most people, meeting them is very dangerous! Better not to confront them directly, but rather to rise above their level by radiating thoughts of love, joy, and peace. Such thoughts align us with the mental plane or higher, and one can trust that some of that bliss will rain down on those denizens of the lower astral who can receive it.

This is the best way to handle your astral initiation: enter the plane at as high a level as possible and transit what remains as quickly as possible. Refuse to see its fabulous vistas as desire forms at all, but as horrors to shun, or as loveliness to be enjoyed without thought of whether you personally

"possess" it or not, just as you can enjoy the beauty of a park without personally owning a title deed to the property. See the astral landscapes as occasions for love, joy, and peace. Then you will actually be living out of a high place in the mental plane, knowing from its more impersonal vantage point the beauty of the upper astral realm and more. The divine power will help all who sincerely yearn for freedom from self to find the upward path.

How might it feel to be on the upper astral level, and then to rise from it to the lower and finally to the upper mental planes? Suppose you have a reasonably pure consciousness, yet are strongly drawn to the warmth of home and family with the security and gratification they bring. You may find yourself, in dream, fantasy, or after-death, in the upper astral in a charming cottage full of light, set in an exquisite garden. It is like a painting by the artist Thomas Kinkade—or like the Shire. You may linger there for a long while amid the comforts of home and the joy of loved ones.

The Third Initiation: Mental

Eventually, however, a moment comes when those persons on the upper astral level realize, with a happy shock of recognition, that they are now so much at home in this circle of light and love, that the need to *depend* on it for security or ego gratification is exhausted. Upon that recognition, they would find themselves living in the same luminous house, in the same timeless circle, but in a new way: on the mental plane rather than the upper astral—for then they would live with the lightness and joy of the truly free, giving and receiving love with shining faces, out of grace rather than need.

The passage from the astral to the mental level, called the "second death" in Theosophy, is like crossing the Ford of Bruinen, leaving behind the ghostly realm of ominous astral encounters for the warm lights of Rivendell, the Last Homely House east of the Sundering Sea. As the Ring party make their way down from Weathertop and approach the ford over the Bruinen River, which will bring them to the Elven haven of Rivendell, the Black Riders grow more and more threatening, even as Frodo, desperately wounded by the grim astral king's blade, grows weaker and weaker. After a final brave defiance of their cries for the Ring as he crosses the raging waters with the foe in pursuit, he swoons and would have fallen into evil hands except that something else happens. The waters rise to a torrent, a shining figure stands on the shore, and the Ringwraiths are carried away by Gandalf's magic. When Frodo awakes, he finds he has been taken into the high home of the fair folk. All he now knows is its peace and fellowship.

In the same way, moving from the upper astral to the mental realm, spiritual travelers will be so much infused with the oneness behind all love that the outer apparent house and garden are no longer necessary to inner completeness, though still there. The travelers will pass as though by easy birth through the second death. They will now be on the lower mental plane, symbolized by Rivendell, in a personal heavenly house built of free, pure, ego-transcended yet still differentiated thought, not tied to emotion or mental desire, but still remaining in the radiation cast by past memories and thought forms.

Finally, the Kinkade-painting house itself may start to fade, until the dweller is living only in the clear ocean of light and love of the formless upper mental plane. The light and love of that plane is so real and immediate that—hard as it is for us to imagine this—it is *more* tangible than any house of stone or friend of flesh. Here are, according to Theosophical sources, formless thoughts and "sweeping" or oceanic experiences of love, beauty, and the divine in their absolute nature, unshaped by human thought or feeling.

As if in analogy to the lower mental sphere, Bilbo says of Rivendell that it is "a perfect house, whether you like food or sleep or story-telling or singing, or just sitting thinking best, or a pleasant mixture of them all"—for "merely to be there was a cure for weariness, fear, and sadness" (1:237). But, as if moving from that to the higher level, Frodo finds as he listens to Elven music that the mystical melodies and swift flowing magical words hold him like an enchantment, even though he grasps little of their meaning. Nonetheless they precipitate into his mind as bright images of realms not seen before on land or sea and as objects never before imagined, until finally they and the hall of the elder kindred all dissolve into a formless maze of even greater glory, like a golden haze over a sunlit sea. Then the otherworldly ocean flows into him to merge with his dreams, to become an undulating light labyrinth, too complex for his mind's eye to follow, but catching him up in its vibrating power till he becomes part of the great dance of the atoms and galaxies, where all memories meet and near and far become one (1:245–6). For in the upper mental plane, the architecture of space and time as we ordinarily know it is transcended, and Hobbits, Elves, and men alike begin to sense the immortal beauty reflecting directly from the One.

Rivendell, reached after the lower astral initiation of Weathertop and the mental plane initiation of the Ford of Bruinen, is pure beauty in its

Rivendell

harmony and diversity, like an ideally balanced mind. It is a palace of memory, where the long-remembering Elves sing of Elbereth and ages past. Also among the guests of Rivendell are the jewel-loving Dwarves, the down-to-earth Hobbits, and embattled men, as though these are all aspects of one's mind. It is finally also a place of decision making and a new start, for after the Council of Elrond, the party of the Ring is formed and departs on December 25. So it is said in Theosophy that, after a restful sojourn on the mental plane (in this connection, called "Devachan"), during which the meaning of the life now past is assimilated on a deep level, one emerges once again to reenter the physical world through birth.

Of course Rivendell, or even Lothlórien, is not fully the mental plane. Its loveliness may be that of the upper astral—this would really depend on the mentality one brought to it. Rivendell is just a corner of the mental plane's wonder, or a metaphor for it. But the Last Homely House suggests especially that plane's timeless beauty, its place above the emotions of this world, its role as a house of remembering and then forgetting, and as a site from which one sets out on a new beginning. As a dwelling place for refuge and hope, Rivendell is like the retreat houses, churches, or temples beloved by some of us as halls of spiritual power from which one can emerge refreshed for the Ring battles of this world.

In this present life, initiations into aspects of the mental plane come whenever we are forced to let go of a special attachment and learn to live in equal relation to all persons and objects. On a small but suggestive scale, we do this frequently. We may have to give up a much loved house or apartment, or to let go of one kind of relationship with a child who has grown and is leaving home for college or marriage. Nearly all of us at some point have had to give up one job for another, or to see a friendship come to an end. On a larger scale, we may have had to go through the tragedy of divorce, or the sorrow of losing a loved one to death.

All such experiences teach us to let go, perhaps through pain, as in all serious initiations, and if we are wise, we will take the opportunity to learn new ways of relating to objects and other persons. Not that we love less, not that we become cold or indifferent, but rather we learn to love more—to relate to a larger circle, to enjoy all places as much as one, to live in a way that is more inclusive and less exclusive. For the more freely one gives love away, the more one has. The more one appreciates wealth and beauty wherever they are and whether one owns them or not, the more wealth and beauty one has. All these opportunities can be like a knock on the door when one is lost in the world of dreams.

We can train ourselves for letting go, which is the key to unlocking mental plane experience. It is for the sake of such training that fasting is recommended in so many spiritual traditions, along with simplicity of life and moderation when one is not fasting. All these are just ways of teaching us that we do not need to *have* in order to enjoy. The idea of possessing stems from astral plane fantasies; now it is time to let them disperse like mists at sunrise. The traditional idea of the Sabbath, of retreats, or of any special religious day is the same: it is a time of training by directing the focus of life to another direction than that of getting, spending, and having.

All these are only beginning initiations. But they are starts, like the wonderful days in Rivendell and Lothlórien on the way to the Cracks of Doom. The pilgrimage goes on, varying between ordeal and rest, each becoming deeper and deeper.

Meditation on Beginning Initiations

Sit quietly. Explore inwardly the physical body and its etheric vitality. Feel its solid form, its vitality, its energy, its potential for the right enjoyment and knowledge of the material world. Hold these experiences for a time.

Then move to the astral plane. Explore the dreamlike or fantasy-like pictures or feelings that come to your mind when you are open to them, or that come unbidden, and are based in feelings and desires. Scan them briefly without attachment from the lowest to the highest. Trace them back to where they came from until you reach the emptiness that is within them, whether they come to you as hollow parasites wanting to draw life from you, or you yourself have projected them onto the blankness.

Finally move your consciousness to the mental plane. See what is there to be appreciated without attachment, and then try to experience something of formless love, light, and divinity, if only a taste. Hold the mind here as long as possible before it sinks back to astral fantasies or physical needs. Then very gently let go of it, but try to keep a bit of the wisdom and loveliness of this exercise always in your consciousness.

Gimli

6

Companions on the Way

All of us humans are unique individuals and at the same time expressions of the universal human, just as we are ourselves and at the same time children of the universe as a whole. Every mother is a mother in her own way. Yet in seeing even the most inexperienced young mother tenderly and instinctively hold her baby, one sees mothers of all times and places, including the great goddesses or the Madonna of Christianity. So it is with figures in *The Lord of the Rings*—each Hobbit, Elf, Dwarf, or man is both an individual and more than a single individual.

In the last chapter we observed that the inhabitants of Rivendell are like aspects of a total personality. All the way through the story, its major characters represent not only themselves, but also something that resonates with one of the general aspects of human and divine consciousness. They are not quite archetypes, for they have very distinct personalities, but each of them—like each of us—is in touch with the archetypes of some particular timeless aspect of universal consciousness and of human nature.

Let us now look sequentially at certain of the principal figures in Tolkien's epic with a view to decoding some of the universal meaning encrypted in each. Other archetypal characters, such as Gandalf, Saruman, and Tom Bombadil, are discussed in other chapters.

Hobbits

In the first chapter we noted that the story's starting-point in the Shire's earthiness and ordinariness makes heroism like that of Frodo and Sam unexpectedly arise from everyday human (or Hobbit) nature. Hobbits represent "everyman" far more than do the men in *The Lord of the Rings*.

The cast of Hobbit characters suggests our experience in another way too, for the wayfarers from the Shire reflect different stages of life. Of the five Hobbits who meet in Rivendell, Bilbo is old, Frodo and Sam are middle-aged, and Merry and Pippin are young. There is rich meaning in each of these three stages.

Bilbo

In Bilbo we see what advanced age really is, a borderline time, ideally bringing in its withered arms all the joy, power, and freedom of being in two worlds at once. Age is not only a time of transitional border-crossing between this life and the next in a linear sense, but far more significantly it can bring years of enhanced awareness of the twin circles within which we live. As one's outer life becomes more limited under the westering sun than it was at high noon, one sees the many colors of sunset reflect even brighter glories just over the margin of this world. One realizes that while slowly bringing to a close one lifetime in this particular corner of space and time, one is also standing in the center of the room, just under the lamp of eternity. In that light, all times are equally real, the timeless archetypes become vivid in dreams and at the back of one's mind, and at moments time itself seems to stop or even to move in other directions than straight ahead. As Bilbo says of his life in Rivendell, "Time doesn't seem to pass here; it just is" (1:243). Of course, for others in that Elvenhome, like Gandalf and Elrond, Rivendell time is tied to an urgent schedule, for the Ring has to be destroyed before it is too late.

But what Bilbo does is simply *be* in that timeless time, remembering. In his memories, the past of a long lifetime merges with the songs about Elbereth and Eärendil that he writes and sings in his thin elderly voice. Finding and keeping the Ring has been the true central task of his life, though it seemed less important to him earlier than it does later, and indeed its full meaning is not understood until much history has passed.

So it may be with many of us: we may have no clear idea at all what, from the point of view of eternity or of all history, was the most important thing we did in life. We may consider our greatest achievements to have been in business or education or creativity. Yet in the end those labors may be as nothing compared to some seemingly more trivial deed, such as befriending an obscure individual or working in an obscure group like the Theosophical Society, the true consequences of which will not be apparent until generations have passed.

Bilbo has to realize, on the other hand, that the part of his life embodying his greatest achievement is behind him. This too is an important realization that comes with age: responsibilities once taken up must be laid down, when the time to hold them has come and gone. Gandalf insists to the old Hobbit, "The Ring has passed on, Bilbo. It would do no good to you or to others, if you tried to meddle with it again" (1:244).

Frodo and Sam

The great responsibility of the Ring has moved into the hands of Hobbits at the height of their powers: Frodo and Sam. They represent mature middle age, taking on the obligation given them in the world in which they are placed. This is the duty and the glory of those midlife years: to know what one must do, and to have the strength and perseverance to do it.

Knowing what to do and having the ability to do it are not easy to come by—no more so than is carrying the Ring. It is, first of all, not always simple to determine just what *I* am supposed to do, and what equally obvious and pressing tasks are not *mine*. For the prime realization that must come to adulthood and that separates it from youth is the deep understanding that one cannot make every choice and take every path. While this fact is outwardly obvious, it may take a while for vital and ambitious persons fully to bring limits into their innermost consciousness.

Middle age does better, however, to do a few things well. Indeed, like Frodo and Sam accompanying him, you may have only *one* overarching task that is laid upon you in this particular lifetime. Whether or not the fate of an entire age and planet rests upon the right performance of that duty, the duty is yours to do. It is said of dharma (the duty given one in a lifetime) that it is better to do your own even imperfectly than to attempt another person's. It is also said that, if you fail in your task, it will remain undone, at least in the special way you would have done it, and that the hole in the world's fabric caused by your undone task will retard the present age until its end.

This is the essence of middle age, that one has certain definite obligations to meet that must not be evaded. Why those obligations come to one person and not to another is a question which, as Gandalf says, cannot be answered. It is, he says, not necessarily because of any superior merit or power that one is chosen over another. If we are chosen, for whatever reason, we must simply respond to the task laid before us with whatever abilities we have (1:70). For as the Wizard further declares, while we may not wish to live in the dark years in which we are placed, the timing is not for us to decide either. The only decision we have is what to do with the time allotted to us (1:60).

MERRY AND PIPPIN

Youth, the time of Merry and Pippin, is the space of freedom before the greatest decisions of life need to be made. The young Hobbits are portrayed as full of laughter and light-hearted jokes, as becomes those without serious responsibility. Their joking play is a gift, because those who do not yet turn the heavy wheels of the world can see its foibles clearly, and it is salutary for all of us that those foibles sometimes be pointed out with humor.

Yet the lively pair also see and hear much that they take seriously. Through the curiosity of the young they have learned, for example, of the Ring before even Frodo tells them of it. They have the foolish impulsiveness of their age, as when Pippin throws a stone into the well in Moria or sneaks a look at the Palantír to Gandalf's dismay. But another side of youth also shines in the two young Hobbits' eyes: the side that is eager to make commitments based on high ideals, together with profound loyalty to friends and those in whom one has placed trust. As Merry, speaking for himself and Pippin, says to Frodo, however great their fear, they want to be with him on his great quest, just as hounds follow their master (1:115–6).

Merry

Chapter Six

Sometimes the world may appear too black-and-white to young people. The virtues of such a stark and simple view are the glue that holds military regiments together and can be used in causes both good and bad. But overall the idealism and friendships of youth represent a consciousness for which one may be nostalgic later on. Combined with characteristic energy and enthusiasm, such idealism and friendship mark an intensity of life that indelibly imprints memory deep down and turns simple events into eternal moments held sacred in one's innermost sanctuary. In this way idealism and friendship help us to see the sacredness of all life and all experience—though occasionally they also bear witness to the need for greater wisdom in directing our energy and enthusiasm.

From the ultimate point of view, however, none of our several ages are *better* as observation points than the others, just different. The jaded eyes of an adult do not necessarily see the world in a way that is wiser or more accurate than the fresh, brightly colored, feeling-laden world of a young person, or even a child. There is enough reality to go around; each wayfarer sees the vista that is opened by the duties, the mental and emotional equipment, and the experience of their current progress along the path of pilgrimage. Everyone's landscape is incomplete but is part of the vast panorama that makes up the full universe with all its planes. In each stage of life the light of the sun, whether of dawn, noon, or eventide, falls in different ways, highlighting different features; only through real spiritual evolution—over one life or many—does one gain vision to perceive more and more segments of reality at once.

Legolas and Gimli

The Elf and Dwarf compan-
ions on the quest indeed widen
the world exemplified in the
Ring-bearer's company. These two
nonhuman individuals represent
high consciousnesses emerging
directly out of nature. In their
woodland and subterranean
lives, with their long separate evolutions, the Elves
and Dwarves have minds
that have taken forms more
directly linked to particular
aspects of the natural world
than the minds of humans or
Hobbits. Elves and Dwarves are like
the devas of Theosophical lore, spirits
on a different evolutionary track from
humans. Their special task is the guard-
ing and guiding of various natural features: trees, mountains, rivers, and seas.
But the Elves and Dwarves of Middle-earth
have nonetheless become independent of
any symbiotic connection to stars or
stones. By the time of *The Lord of the
Rings*, they "have their own labours
and their own sorrows" (1:94),
though they retain the long memory

Legolas

of nature. Likewise, their love of the underground labyrinths or sylvan glades, in which they first glimpsed the beauty and breathed the sweet air of earth at the Beginning, bespeaks the rock and the wood from which they were hewn.

The Elves seem like the fairies or sylphs of traditional lore. They are "elementals" or conscious expressions of air and woods. But they show the

Gimli

rich potential of natural consciousness as they let its awareness grow within them to a wisdom often exceeding that of men and women.

The Dwarves are no doubt the gnomes of tradition, "elementals" of earth and familiars of caves and mines. Their consciousness has the weight, the tenacity, and the dark secret loves of the roots of mountains. These two races, mistrustful of one another for ages, are reconciled in the growing friendship of Legolas and Gimli.

As possessors of natural consciousness raised to a high degree, each race understands its element profoundly enough to create marvelous works of art: the jeweled Silmarilli of the Eldar Elves, gleaming in the sunlight, and the wondrously wrought swords and armor of the Dwarves. Yet Elves and Dwarves are not of humankind or Hobbitkind: "Our paths cross theirs seldom, by chance or purpose," says the Elf Gildor (1:94). And the early history of the Dwarves is not well known by any of the larger folk.

As represented by Legolas and Gimli, these races are important members of the mission sent to destroy the Ring, for they, as well as all other free folk, will be enslaved by the Dark Lord if the Ring's terrible magic finds its way into his possession. In the cooperation of Elf and Dwarf, we see, as if in a parable, that the powers of nature, including the highest natural consciousnesses, are not at odds with each other or with humanity—though sometimes they may seem to be. Rather all nature must cooperate against evils that threaten to make all beings only twisted distortions of their original pattern.

If nature is reduced to slavery under any entity that is, in the words of Tom Bombadil, "filled with a hatred of things that go free upon the earth" (1:141), then nature is not what it was meant to be, a realm with a life of its own apart from any purpose imposed upon it by humans or other overlords. If nature is not allowed to be what it is in its own right, neither are humans able rightly to fulfill their role as nature's priests and caretakers, for like the Elves and Tom, humans are meant to enjoy and enrich nature's beauty by art, but not to diminish its selfhood.

Galadriel

The Elven Queen of Lothlórien, whom the Ring companions find beautiful beyond all imagining, able even to melt the heart of Gimli the Dwarf to her love and service, stands as the Woman of the Stars, the transcendent protector unstained by any evil of this world, and the last hope past any despair here below. She is archetypically one with Wisdom or Sophia in the Book of Proverbs ("Wisdom has built her house . . . she calls from the highest places in the town" 9.1, 3) and with the Blessed Virgin Mary in the traditional Roman Catholic piety that Tolkien himself espoused throughout his life.

Galadriel as archetype of the divine feminine can also be assimilated to Elbereth or Gilthoniel, spouse of the Lord of the Valar, who fashioned this world ("Ages ago I [Wisdom] was set up, at the first, before the beginning of the earth" Prov. 8.23). Galadriel, the present Queen of Lothlórien, had lived long ago in the Undying Lands under the rule of Elbereth, to whom she sang a sweet and sad lament for those golden shores "Beyond the Sun, Beyond the Moon" (1:389).

It is the powerful name of Elbereth that most benefits Frodo when he is under siege by the Ringwraiths on Weathertop. Similarly, when the Ring-bearer and Sam perilously enter the heart of darkness in Cirith Ungol, Frodo takes the phial of clear light given him by Galadriel and, thrusting it into his bosom, holds it next to his heart. Its faint but unfailing light from eternal beauty sustains the two small adventurers as they venture farther and farther into the depths of evil. Several times, in fact, her light shows their way and repels minions of darkness in that terrible place. When bestowing this gift upon him, Galadriel promised Frodo that its light would shine all the brighter the darker the night, becoming, in words Sam remembers when all is indeed midnight in Cirith Ungol, "*a light when all other lights go out*." As the blackness looms huge about him, he sees in his mind something like a miniature portrait of Galadriel on the sunlit green grass of Lorien, with gifts in her hand (1:395, 2:329).

Tolkien would probably have been hard at work on the last chapters of the novel in 1950, that coldest of all Cold War years, a time that looked dark for the free peoples and the Western alliance, from Korea to Washington. It was also the year in which Pope Pius XII, a pontiff who set his face firmly against evil spreading from the East, defined the dogma of the Assumption of the Blessed Virgin Mary into Heaven. The religious spirit of that event in those desperate days feels somehow convergent with the hope called up by the Queen of Lothlórien. The Catholic convert and novelist Graham Greene wrote of that year in a popular magazine, "Sometimes it seems as though the supernatural were gathering its forces for our support, and whom should we expect in the vanguard but Our Lady?" (*Life*, October 30, 1950, p. 56).

The party has to leave Galadriel's realm, for as she says, they have chosen, and the tides of fate are flowing (1:381). But they leave on their quest as knights in her service.

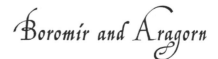

Boromir and Aragorn

The two men in the Ring party are contrasting figures who suggest the two levels of human nature, the lower and the higher.

Boromir

Boromir corresponds to the lower human nature, called in Theosophy the lower quaternity, which is the human expression of the four lower planes of the manifested universe presented in the preceding chapter: the physical, etheric, astral, and lower mental.

The lower mental "body," which is closely linked to our earthly life and physical form, is usually not highly developed as an expression of love and the divine. It lacks that development because its link with the energies of the higher Self, which would awaken those realizations, is frequently

Boromir

94

blocked. For most of us, most of the time, especially in everyday life apart from dreams and meditation, the lower mental is simply the ordinary mind—remembering, instinctive, problem-solving, and generally well interfused with astral desire-based energy. The lower mental is above the astral desire plane only in the sense that it has full conscious self-awareness and rationality. But the life of pure reason is not easy to attain without help from that which is above reason.

So is the case with Boromir. The great warrior from Gondor, who tries to wrest the Ring from Frodo, considers himself devoted to high principles of honor, love of country, and hatred of evil. Yet all this in fact is intermixed with the kind of pride that is really attachment to self. All self-attachment comes down to desire, power, and fear: desire for power to fend off that which we fear. What we fear most deeply is dissolution of the self, or of outer projections like wealth, rank, and nation, which symbolize the integrity of self to us. So Boromir, centered in the lower quaternity, thinks much of his fine manly body, its martial prowess, and the etheric sheen that bespeaks its valor and vitality.

He wants the Ring, he tells himself, only so that he can use it for the salvation of his country, for the sake of good (1:414). But then the other face of the Ring's power speaks through him: "It might have been mine. It should be mine. Give it to me!" (1:415). But Frodo, though desperate at this assault by the much larger and stronger man, knows well, as does Gandalf, that such a "gift" will corrupt strength and lead only to further evil.

Actions of the lower quaternity, being in the realm of cause and effect, have repercussions through what is called "karma." One does not escape receiving back in some form what one has sent out into the universe by all one's thoughts, words, and deeds, whether benign or ill. Shortly after trying to seize possession of Frodo's burden, Boromir dies heroically trying to save the other Hobbits from Orcs. Something in him rises to karmic awareness as he dies, and virtually his last words are, "I tried to take the Ring from Frodo. . . . I am sorry. I have paid" (2:16).

Chapter Six

Aragorn

Aragorn, on the other hand, is presented as always wiser, less impulsive, more considered in his judgments, than the man of Gondor. The link to his higher Self is relatively more open. The higher Self, or higher triad, consists of Atma, Buddhi, and Manas. Starting with the last, "Manas" refers to what is described in the previous chapter as the upper mental plane, the lofty formless consciousness of light and love as virtually tangible realities. "Buddhi" is essentially this level of awareness taken to universal dimensions. It is what is sometimes called cosmic consciousness and is roughly what the Buddhists call Nirvana.

Buddhi, however, is also the ultimate source of realization and creative intuition, as it reflects down into the mental plane. All real creativity is simply putting together two or more things that no one had thought of putting together before: musical notes in a new composition, colors and forms in a work of art, ideas or possible actions in business or statesmanship. Seeing things come together stems, at the deepest or highest level, from consciousness of the divine oneness of all that exists, for that is the supreme "putting together." Therefore to be open to buddhic consciousness is not only to contemplate the inexpressible bliss of high beingness, but also to tap into a fountainhead of creativity, which can shower down into our everyday mind and action.

"Atma" is the ultimate level of the higher Self, Brahman or God—the oneness of the buddhic cosmic consciousness taken to the point of realizing that it is also divine consciousness. Within the self, Atma, with Buddhi as its "vehicle," is the monad, the pilgrim, traveling as an expression of the divine through countless worlds and lifetimes till it finally returns again, enriched by all it has seen, to the Light, which is its true home.

In short, to be one with the higher Self, even intuitively and without necessarily having the "right" names to attach to it, is to act out of love and universality, free of obtrusive regard for the separate self. The higher Self is like an outpost of this fundamental reality within each of us. When it informs our thoughts, our pilgrimage may take us on far journeys, but always for a purpose: as is said of Strider, the name by which the Hobbits first know Aragorn, "Not all those who wander are lost" (1:182).

Aragorn, as a practical man, does not talk about a connection to the higher Self so much as he expresses it in action. Expressing oneness at ground level, he works always with regard to the greater good, toward which he can smile and subordinate himself. And like all true knowers of the higher Self, he knows how to keep silent. Gandalf calls him "the greatest traveller and huntsman of this age of the world" (1:67). That could be taken to mean one liberated from attachment to time and place, and whose eye, unclouded by ego, sees all things as they really are.

The White Crown

Strider-Aragorn says that he and his companion rangers protect the ordinary men and Hobbits of the Shire and Bree without their knowing it and without desire for respect or reward. That is the way the higher Self acts, shining like the sun far above the self-centeredness of the lower self. If the object is to keep those who are small and defenseless free from fear or abuse, they have to be kept innocent of both the dangers around them and the labors of their guardians. For if they know they are being shielded, they will also know dread (1:261–2).

When Aragorn becomes King Elessar of Gondor and the West, his coronation rightly symbolizes the proper ascendancy of the higher Self over the lower self.

Gollum

This shrunken Hobbit-like creature, whose real name is Sméagol and whom Sam also calls Slinker and Stinker, represents the small pathetic face of evil. Wickedness, however splendid its trumpet blasts before the world, however grand the boasting pride of Satan or Sauron, ends up showing the emptiness of its dark towers when it finds its own true level: as meanness in petty creatures, as frightened children and devastated homes. Yet, in one of Tolkien's most brilliant turns, Gollum also tells us of the way in which all beings, however perverted, may yet have a role to play for good in the overall pattern of the universe—for even the wise do not know all ends.

Gollum is clearly a creature utterly twisted by one thing, his addictive attachment to the Ring. He is turned upon himself, unable to feel or truly know another being because of his utter preoccupation with that single desire—with one recorded exception, as we shall see, for nothing is *absolutely* evil. His lust leads him to follow after the Ring party, and for a time even to help and guide them. No doubt he also hopes somehow to be able to grab back that which he calls his "Precious." One theme in the novel may be symbolic of the way in which, of the two possessors of the Ring, Gollum and Frodo, the latter has greater strength to resist its corrupting power. Both receive the Ring on their birthday: Gollum by means of theft and murder, though he later claims it was his rightful present; Frodo as a genuine gift from Bilbo, however reluctantly given.

On a certain occasion reminiscent of the much earlier homicide, after a long debate with himself, Gollum reaches out toward the sleeping Ring-bearer's neck with intent to kill, only to be stopped by Sam (2:241). And indeed he does seize the enchanted Ring at the very end, by biting off Frodo's finger. Yet without him that dread Power would not have been destroyed, for Frodo at the last minute cannot bring himself to

throw his burden into the Cracks of Doom. So Gandalf's earlier wisdom and pity, in letting Gollum live, allow the justice of the universe to move forward in unforeseen ways.

There are grounds to pity the poor creature as well as for revulsion. On another occasion, in one of the most poignant episodes in the book, as Frodo, Sam, and Gollum make their torturous way toward the mountain of destiny, Gollum seems to find something of affection, even of love, in his twisted heart—for no creature, however debased, is without the higher Self somewhere within. Utterly exhausted and made spiritless by the sullen, smoky terrain through which they struggle toward Mordor, the three travelers rest. Frodo and Sam slide into sleep, while Gollum watches warily.

Then, for one blessed moment, Gollum eases himself up to Frodo and gently puts out a tenuous, unsteady hand toward the knee of the sleeping Hobbit he calls master. It is almost as though he were, for the first time in countless years, touching another being with tenderness. For an instant he is not the starved and bitter slave of the Ring, but just another aging Hobbit like the one to whom he is reaching out. He is bent and wary, but not beyond a sense of kinship for those with whom he is bound up in the bundle of life and in the sharing of their common obsession.

Then Frodo stirs, and "the fleeting moment had passed, beyond recall." Sam awakens, calls out roughly to the intruder who murmurs "Nice Master!" but withdraws into himself, crouching and looking "almost spider-like," muttering again under his breath at the world's hardness.

Gollum shows, in extreme degree, that we can be twisted almost beyond return, yet still retain within ourselves a glint of the divine light— and the ability, willing or not, to do something that advances the divine plan.

Meditation Guided by the Companions

Sit quietly, still the mind.

Then scan the different planes or "bodies" within yourself. Get in touch again with the lower quaternity of the physical, etheric, astral, and lower mental planes. As you do so, analyze yourself to see what in you might keep you trapped, like Boromir or Gollum, on one or another of them.

Then, going deeper, seek to arouse awareness of the higher Self. You may not actually enter it in full consciousness, but be attuned to its luminous presence within, or see it symbolized by the beauty and power of Galadriel, or by that part of yourself that is greater than your present age or this particular lifetime alone. Seek to strengthen that light so as to clear the channels between the higher Self and the lower self within, so that the latter is more and more guided by the divine.

Then, stilling the mind even more, experience at least a touch of the higher triad: the mental plane, the buddhic cosmic and intuitive consciousness, and the monad on pilgrimage within you. They express the divine One above, beyond, and within all the ages and kindred in the universe—reflected in ourselves.

As you return gradually and gently to ordinary consciousness, resolve to make yourself an intentional instrument of the divine plan, and of the work of light and love in the world.

7

The Great Initiation

The climax of *The Lord of the Rings* comes when the Ring-bearer proceeds into the heart of the Enemy's land alone, save for one faithful companion, Sam. There his dreadful burden must be destroyed at the forge of its making. That cauldron of beginnings and endings is the fiery Cracks of Doom, where the shaping, melting powers of earth on all planes are most concentrated and rage upwards to the world's surface.

The terrible journey begins the same day as Boromir's attempt to seize the Ring from Frodo and that impulsive warrior's subsequent heroic death at the hands of the Orcs. Putting on the Ring to make himself invisible, the solitary Hobbit takes a boat to cross the river onto the Mordor side, knowing the mission is then in his hands alone. He has to complete it unaided, or perish in the attempt.

However, Sam catches up with his master and joins him; the Ring-bearer is both appalled and delighted to find he is not by himself after all. The two proceed through the hard barrens of Emyn Muil, where the former possessor of the Ring, Gollum, pursues them until captured and made to serve as their guide. That sniveling Hobbit-like creature takes them across the dead marshes toward Cirith Ungol, a secret passageway into the Land of Shadows.

On the way they encounter Faramir in the once fair land of Ithilien. There, amidst the enemy, this younger brother of Boromir and his band have a secret outpost. The Hobbits and men exchange news of Boromir and of the War. Frodo and Sam then continue on. In the cave passageways of Cirith Ungol, the two intruders from the Shire enter the lair of Shelob, a gigantic spider of unfathomable evil. She paralyzes Frodo before Sam is able to dispatch her.

Sam has to take the Ring and decide whether to continue alone or to try to carry Frodo, not sure whether his master is alive or dead. Orcs then seize the inert body of the former owner of Bag End. Sam finally rescues Frodo and returns the dreadful burden of the Ring, after which the pair plod on in the increasingly weary and seemingly hopeless trek to the one place where the Ring can be destroyed.

As they approach Mount Doom, the Ring grows more and more on Frodo's mind even as all his normal senses sink into a black fog: "I am naked in the dark, Sam, and there is no veil between me and the wheel of fire. I begin to see it even with my waking eyes, and all else fades" (3:215).

The pair arrive at the burning abyss, deep in the volcanic heart of the dark smoking mountain where the Ring was made. But Frodo, finally under the Ring's full dominion, now refuses to destroy it. Instead, he puts on the evil device. Then Gollum, also recklessly impassioned by the tiny circle glowing like bright fire at the place of its highest power, rushes toward him. The maddened little creature fights with his master's invisible form and gains the dread circlet for himself by biting off Frodo's finger. But as he dances with glee, holding his "Precious" high in the turbid air, he topples into the fiery crevice, obliterating both himself and the object of his desire. The Ring is annihilated, and the power of the Dark Tower is vanquished.

This final effort amounts to an initiation for both Frodo and Sam. For the Ring-bearer himself the initiation is not entirely successful, since he could

not bring himself to do what was to be the fulfillment of his quest by casting the Ring into the fire. So the work is unintentionally finished by one thought to be an enemy. Nevertheless, the powerful forces generated by the initiatory ordeal bear him and the other players in the final act along to its conclusion. Though Frodo is by now beyond a will of his own, the drama itself leads them all to complete together the labor originally laid upon him alone.

Perhaps we too, at least once or twice in our lives, have undergone what may be considered a major initiation, and it may have seemed no less heroic, terrible, and ambiguous than Frodo's. Like him, after we have been through it, we may have experienced power and been changed, yet we may also know we did not always act worthily during the ordeal, and feel diffident when praised. If any good came from this, even to the doer—we tell ourselves—it was not my weak self, but something mysterious and greater than myself working through me that accomplished it: I just happened to be there.

The event we are considering is not one of those minor initiatory experiences that are half ceremonial, or even one of those—like birth, puberty, entering the adult world, or death itself—that are difficult, though common to all humankind in some form. The kind of initiation we are now thinking of is not only difficult but, in some important way, uniquely our own. It may have been a very serious illness or injury, or a torturous relationship that had to be worked through for the sake of our own peace and that of others. Perhaps an extremely demanding task was clearly laid upon us as a dharma or calling: a dangerous but important mission in wartime or a thankless peacetime job offering only much sacrifice and bringing bitter animosity from the many who misunderstand. Or the initiation may be an inward mission of no less peril and promise: painful but necessary growth or change within oneself; as such, it could involve overcoming an addiction, transforming attitudes toward others, changing attitudes toward oneself, or mastering the dark inner clouds of depression or anger.

When does the heart of an initiation begin? It starts when the candidate is separated from all others or from all but a single companion, who may represent an aspect of the candidate's own self, and when the candidate must meet that which is "other" face to face. It is the state of the medieval servant of chivalry at the heart of his initiation into knighthood, spending a night in solitary vigil in the chapel. Or it may be the Native American youth separating himself even from other novices to go on the vision quest or spend days in the sweat lodge, remaining alone, fasting and waiting until his individual deity appears. Or again, if there is a companion, it is like Tamino and Pamina in Mozart's opera *The Magic Flute*, holding hands as they pass through various horrific initiatory hells and purgatories reminiscent of the lower astral realm.

In *The Lord of the Rings*, the "inner" initiation within the greater commences when Frodo realizes that, because of the Ring, evil in the person of Boromir has entered even into the company of the Nine Walkers. Not wanting to risk those dearest to him in what now seems virtually a hopeless quest, he resolves to go at once, and alone (1:417–8). Putting on the Ring to vanish from the others, Frodo sets out in a boat for the far side of the river. That distant shore is the evil side, the quest side, of the sundering stream.

As so often happens in life, the separation that is the beginning of an intense, climactic initiatory ordeal is not planned. While there may have been a vague idea that sometime the breaking of the fellowship would come, it is only the unanticipated events of one day that impel the decisive event to occur under that same sun.

For us, too, major initiations are probably not programmatic, like those of life stages or spiritual office, but are forced upon us by outer events. The sickness comes, the job that must be done is laid before us by another or by the times themselves, the catastrophe hits, the winds of war or fate blow wildly and send in our direction that for which perhaps we were born, but do not welcome. For this is initiation by events or by the mysterious course of a life, not a simulated ordeal from an intentional scenario—as helpful as dramatized initiations may be in preparing one for the real thing.

The willingness to face the trial alone is the first test, and that test Frodo passes as his boat with himself as its invisible helmsman slips into the dark waters. We have noted before that the fourth initiation, as described by C. W. Leadbeater, entails above all the dread and terror, perhaps unimaginable by most of us amid our people- and work-cluttered lives, of being utterly and absolutely alone in the face of an ultimate trial. But this is what Frodo is now entering upon, and he knows it. As he is fully aware, inwardly he is alone even after Sam and Gollum join his final trek toward the Mountain of Doom.

Virtually as reward for his solitary venture, the Ring-bearer gains Sam as his continuing companion when the faithful servant leaps into the bark just as it leaves the shore. But it is still he alone who—by now almost always—has the Ring in his mind as a wheel of fire, a circle of destiny. He alone feels its ominous and increasing weight as he plods along with that burden despite extremes of hunger, thirst, weariness, and fear of the searching Eye, which wants above all that which he bears. He alone suffers in grotesque internal conflict, which makes him both want to surrender it to its maker and strengthens him in his resolve that the searching Eye must not have it.

At the commencement of our own initiations, when we feel ourselves most alone in our difficult passage, another may unexpectedly appear to stand with us. We too may go through times when all seems hopeless and we feel utterly unloved, unwanted, and left to ourselves. But ordeals are likely to combine awesome tribulations with an occasional encouraging respite. You, too, may find a helper as you set out on an inner journey of initiation, and Frodo could not have completed his duty without Sam or even, as it turned out, that other and much less desired companion, Gollum. Yet at the same time, we know the initiation is something that only we can bear, and so it must be borne alone.

The sort of major initiation in one's life of which we are speaking begins in a situation that is experienced as extremely difficult and painful either physically or mentally or in both ways. It is not a gradual, steady progression to greater and greater light, much less a sudden revelation of glory. Those mystical exaltations may happen, and those who experience them have much for which to be thankful, but such exaltations are not initiatory experiences in the classic sense. Delights may occur along the initiatory road, like the companions' visits to Rivendell and Lothlórien, but the road itself will also offer many hard stretches, above all at the beginning and just before the end.

The first trial, as indicated, is the inner aloneness. You are now entering a way of being in the world that sets you apart from your associates, even those nearest and dearest. What you are entering is a real-life passion play that you realize you must face for yourself, by yourself, and there is little point in talking much about it, for no one else can really understand your deeply personal version of the eternal drama. C. W. Leadbeater's account of the fourth initiation is clearly parallel to both the crucifixion of Christ and Frodo's ordeal on Mount Doom, being marked by profound and terrible aloneness, together with abuse by those around. In the harsh light of the changed realities, even once congenial surroundings take on a grim, prison-like cast, once friendly faces look mocking and censorious, and one must find a new way of walking among them—with a single companion, if one is fortunate, and perhaps also with one's own personal Gollum as an unwilling helper.

Chapter Seven

So it is that, after landing on the disorienting steppes of Emyn Muil, Frodo and Sam have to find their way anew. They have not been there before: the arena of their major initiation is unfamiliar. At first, the two small Hobbits wander through thunder-racked hills and reeking marshes without a clear sense of direction, but feeling all too keenly the ominous, inhospitable character of the vast uncharted terrain around them. Still they know that they have to reach the heart of this abomination before they can return.

Ordinary compasses do not work amid the sinister magnetism of such a place at such a time, and footing is unsure. The labyrinthine initiatory paths are unmarked, the landscape looks stony and forbidding, and the air is stormy and shadowy.

The necessary guide comes in the form of Sméagol, now known as Gollum, the wizened hungry creature who was once the keeper of the Ring. He is drawn to Frodo and Sam by his continuing sleeping and waking dreams of its fiery circle, and after his capture he promises to guide them truly, swearing on the one thing that really binds him—the "Precious" itself.

As one enters into a major initiation, much may be stirred up, both positive and negative, and Gollums may be pulled toward us. The magnetic, evil power in the Ring grows greater and greater as the abyss of fire where it was crafted comes nearer and danger increases. In such a situation, the Gollums in one's life, the shadow-sides of obsessions and commitments, will be aroused and must be tamed.

With the best, there is also the shadow of something bad. With staunch faith, there is the risk of fanaticism; with deep love, possessiveness. Our inner Gollums are always wanting to whittle down any virtue to the hunger of the lean half-starved Sméagol-soul. But the fates of our Gollums can also be put on fast-forward, leading to ultimate outcomes that are at first unknown. We may suddenly realize how to sublimate what has seemed an inner negative energy into great power for good, or we may learn, as did Frodo and Sam, that pity for even the most despicable creature is not wasted.

It is noteworthy also that Frodo earlier told Gollum in an uncharacteristic commanding voice that he would never get his "Precious" back again. The Ring-bearing Hobbit even brags to his pitiful companion that, if he has to, he can put on the Ring and command Gollum to jump from a cliff or leap into a fire, and he will do it (2:248).

Are these awesome words a curse, a prophecy, or just a statement of fact? Whatever the case may be, they foretell the future at the Cracks of Doom—except that it is not by any command Frodo utters, but as a consequence of Frodo's having been himself overmastered by the Ring, that Gollum is cast into the fire. It is the desire for the Precious that betrays them both, yet also it is that desire which destroys its own object.

We might say that even our weaknesses together with those of others around us—codependents, in the current jargon—can sometimes work a dangerous judo that brings us to victory in the end despite ourselves. Alcoholics Anonymous says that problem drinkers may have to "hit bottom"—get into a situation in which, despite extreme reluctance, they are forced to recognize the devastating impact of their addiction—before they seek help that can be effective. There are easier ways to be freed from self-forged chains, but if nothing else works, the fatal attraction itself may have to leverage a turning around and destroy itself, as though it were one's own Precious. Even if achieved without our conscious participation, this process is nonetheless an initiation.

The episode in the westward-facing caves with Faramir and his companions is a respite in the midst of an initiatory ordeal. In ours, too, a brief or partial return to ordinary life is possible: a remission in the illness, a short leave from war, or a weekend away from the crisis. One sees the faces of people not involved in the ordeal and hears their voices; one views something of old familiar sites and even tastes regular food. But the tension of the initiatory ordeal remains in the background . . . one is always aware of it. The crisis is the subject of much conversation, because it is the battle that all whom one meets are also fighting, each in their own way.

Chapter Seven

After Ithilien comes the heart of the initiation for Frodo and Sam in the fearful winding caverns of Cirith Ungol. Its events are classic initiatory features: the winding underground passageway, fighting and finally slaying the monster, apparent death and return to new life. The very antiquity of the story, as old as the Labyrinth and the Minotaur, reminds us of what Sam realizes, that this is a tale coming to us from out of the past, a tale which we are now living and which will continue long after us. The single crisis we face is not the beginning or the end of the tale, nor is it our own beginning or end. We play our part, but the reverse of our present role will be the next part we play. After the fear and passion of battle, the subsequent scene is set amid the calm of victory or death; after victory, comes the next struggle; after death, new life. Let the story sing in you as

Orcs

you enact it, let it not seem to end, for it will not end in our age of the world, or for many ages to come.

In the grisly depths of Cirith Ungol, Frodo's body, poisoned by Shelob, is captured by Orcs. This foul brood of creatures are servants of Sauron, first bred by Morgoth at the beginning of the wars between Elves and the Witch-king. From what stock they came is not known, but it is worth noting that, like Sauron himself, their progenitors were not originally as they now are: "The Shadow that bred them can only mock, it cannot make: not real new things of its own. I don't think it gave life to the Orcs, it only ruined them and twisted them" (3:190).

Their twisting not only makes them apt to evil, it also weakens them. For the Orcs' ill nature leads them to fight among themselves as much as against the foes of the Darkness that they serve. The Orcs seem never to have a good word to say about one another. They continually denigrate, threaten, and quarrel, and are as likely to betray their comrades as not. Because they serve their Nazgûl masters and the Dark Lord out of fear rather than love, only whips and curses maintain what little order these goblins have.

The Orcs within each of us are no different. The various lusts, fears, angers, and lassitudes that want to paralyze or divert our progress toward initiation can fight fiercely for control over us. But they are no less at war with each other. A moment's thought will remind us that every inner Orc is at odds with every other, and if any of them should manage to take over the driver's seat, it would quickly either be overthrown by a fellow goblin or smash up the vehicle. To live only for anger at someone or some situation will undercut one's lust for money or love; one's obsessive fears will mock one's drive for power or fame.

If one single inner Orc does manage to stay in charge for any length of time, its host will soon find that there can never be enough food, drink, sex, or power to satisfy that demon, and the effort to satisfy it will darken the mind and then destroy one's life. Moreover, though Orcs may try to tell us that they represent freedom and that morality and the spiritual path are slavery, they themselves are in a far more abject bondage than the saint, as they labor for "fulfillment" under the whip of mindless biological impulses or psychological reactions. They are bred in the lower self as it twists into devils what are in themselves wholesome instincts, but they can be subdued by the radiance of the higher Self, like Shelob wounded by the bright light of Galadriel's phial.

Finally, after escape from the Orcs, the last ordeal of this particular chapter of our personal story arrives at the Cracks of Doom. This is the climax of Frodo's initiation, the moment when the task is completed, the Ring destroyed, and the protagonist transformed into the heroic yet oddly luminous, almost otherworldly, figure he becomes. Yet, as we know, something very strange happens at that climactic moment.

Frodo fails the supreme test. He is unable to cast the Ring into the Cracks of Doom. Instead he puts it on his own finger, saying, "I have come.

Defeat of the Nazgûl Chieftain

. . . But I do not choose now to do what I came to do. I will not do this deed. The Ring is mine!" (3:223). This is, of course, not really a choice, but the result of the complete destruction of his will by the overwhelming power of the Ring in that place and at that moment.

As Frodo slips the Ring on, we are told that the Dark Tower is shaken, the Dark Lord is suddenly aware of the Ring-bearer, "and his Eye piercing all shadows looked across the plain to the door that he had made" (3:223), as he realizes his folly. The Ringwraiths dash toward the Mountain in a flurry of wings: there is a rival to the Master of the Dark Tower, and for them mortal danger.

What would have happened next, if the Hobbit from the Shire had continued to wear the instrument of world power, we can only speculate, for he does not keep it long. An even less likely contestant for the dark empire of Middle-earth seizes it merely a moment later, leaving its claimant to be

Chapter Seven

"Frodo of the Nine Fingers"—a title at once of heroism and failure. For all his unworthiness and without intending it, Gollum is necessary to complete the task.

Our own major initiations may have much in common with Frodo's. We too can find that, at the end, we fail in an important part of the initiation's inner as well as outer work, yet somehow the destiny laid upon us in the first place takes over, and the work is completed, perhaps through an unexpected agency—even by the unwilling assistance of one who outwardly has appeared to be an enemy. For even the wise do not see all ends.

It may be that, if the trial is pain or illness, we do not always bear it with good grace, but fall into complaining at the world's injustice, rage against that which has laid us low, or fall into deep depression over our fate. We are not always heroic. Yet nonetheless the ordeal is completed, we survive and are at least partially healed, and may emerge on the other side changed, a new person. As so often is the case with those who have long lived with pain or death, we emerge a gentler, more compassionate individual, like Coleridge's Ancient Mariner, who after his terrible testing at sea was able softly to say, "He prayeth best who loveth best, all things both great and small." So it is with Frodo after the Cracks of Doom. He becomes a specially marked, unworldly seeming Hobbit, not meant to remain long in this rough world. That is perhaps the reward for his heroism in most of his labors and is also no doubt due to the humbling—one might even say, salutary and needful humbling—effect of his one great failure.

And it may be that aid comes at the time of crisis from one we did not consider would have such a part in our own drama: a doctor we think unhelpful, or an acquaintance or relative we regard as unsympathetic, perhaps rightly so, but who intentionally or not says or does the one thing needful. However it happens, the ordeal comes to a sudden end, the strife is over, and victory is achieved—until the next chapter in the story.

Meditation on the Great Initiation

Quiet your mind. Then bring up images of the most difficult and life-changing event that has happened to you. Trace its sequence from start to finish. If you feel led to do so, and can do so without unneeded pain, relive the event in your mind and feelings.

Next focus on the few words, the idea, or the picture in your mind that best sums up the essence or meaning of that event. Do not think about or analyze the words or picture, but just hold them or it in your mind. Just hear the words or gaze at the object. Let the attention you pay quiet your stream of consciousness.

Then let even those words or that picture disappear so that you are mentally gazing into the still emptiness that lies behind all the words and images. Absorb the bliss and perspective it gives.

Then slowly, carefully, bring your mind back to ordinary consciousness. But let the experience of again seeing this decisive event stay with you throughout the day. Let any new meanings or understandings that may come out of it seep into your conscious awareness, and learn from them as the day goes forward. Try to learn also from what lies behind all events on the surface of the world.

by callahan 2004

8

From Middle-earth to the Undying Lands

After the destruction of the Ring, the story commences a long, slow winding down. The tranquillity and leisure of travels and events as the companions journey homeward contrast mightily with the building anxiety of the outward venture. Only upon their return to the beloved Shire do the Hobbits find fresh evil, though now on a petty scale, that has to be dealt with.

We read that in the Field of Cormallen, with the loss of central leadership from the Dark Tower, the Nazgûl and their armies collapse. Then, as events move in swift and joyous succession, Frodo and Sam are welcomed to Gondor with exalted praise, Faramir as the last Steward of the realm yields to Aragorn, who is now to rule as the rightful King Elessar. At his coronation, Gandalf places the crown on the sovereign's head. The new monarch is shortly after married to the fair Arwen, daughter of the Elf-lord Elrond.

Frodo and Sam, together with Merry, Pippin, Gandalf, and the other companions, join Elrond's party as it proceeds back to Rivendell, first

Chapter Eight

accompanying the King of the Mark to Rohan, where he remains, then visiting the scene of the great battle at Helm's Deep. They also call at Isengard, Saruman's ruined stronghold, where the exchange between Gandalf and his erstwhile Wizard colleague reveals only the latter's smallness and bitterness in defeat. Proceeding to Bree, they chat with Barliman, the innkeeper, who is, needless to say, astounded at the turn of events, above all at the man he knew as Strider, a somewhat disreputable Ranger, becoming a mighty king.

Returning to the Shire, the four Hobbits quickly grasp that much has gone wrong. In an account reminiscent of the gloomiest descriptions of the industrial revolution together with twentieth-century totalitarianism, a new "order" had arrived, bringing pollution, the desecration of all that was green and fair, and the virtual enslavement of the once jovial, easy-going Hobbits to endless rules and harsh masters. Before long they learn that Saruman, who has meanwhile progressed to the Shire and is still capable of small-scale knavery, is behind it all. Driving him out, the returned Hobbit adventurers set matters to right.

Once that task is accomplished, wonder days begin in the Shire. With the help of a handful of miraculous dust given to him by Galadriel, Sam's gardens grow with glorious abundance, trees shoot up almost overnight, the great damage done to the Shire is healed, and even the children born that marvelous year, 1420 by Shire Reckoning, "were fair to see and strong." Indeed, in that year, "Not only was there wonderful sunshine and delicious rain, in due times and perfect measure, but there seemed something more: an air of richness and growth, and a gleam of a beauty beyond that of mortal summers that flicker and pass upon this Middle-earth" (3:303). That year is also famous for its weddings; in the spring, Sam marries Rose Cotton. Their first child, Elanor, is born on March 25 of the following year, a day Frodo notes, for he is ill around that time, which is the anniversary of the destruction of the Ring.

His illness is a sign to Frodo that his life in Middle-earth is ending; though his deed has led to this fabulous climax, he himself is too wounded by the struggle to continue on this side of the Sundering Sea. Sam then tells him, with tears in his eyes, that he expected him to live in the Shire, enjoying a life of well-earned honor and comfort, for many years to come. But Frodo answers that, although he also once thought so, he now realizes that he has been too deeply hurt for that kind of gentle retirement. He has saved the Shire for others, not for himself. "It must often be so, Sam, when things are in danger: some one has to give them up, lose them, so that others may keep them" (3:309). (Tolkien himself had fought in World War I, in which, he later said, he lost all but one of his friends; he knew well the meaning of such sacrifice.)

Chapter Eight

So it is that when autumn comes, Frodo leaves for the Grey Havens, joined by Elrond, Galadriel, and many other Elves of the high kindred, as well as Gandalf. Their work in Middle-earth is finished. To Frodo's immense surprise and delight, Bilbo is also in the party from Rivendell that sails away from the last haven of Middle-earth. "And the ship went out into the High Sea and passed on into the West, until at last on a night of rain Frodo smelled a sweet fragrance on the air and heard the sound of singing that came over the water. And then it seemed to him that as in his dream in the house of Bombadil, the grey rain-curtain turned all to silver glass and was rolled back, and he beheld white shores and beyond them a far green country under a swift sunrise" (3:310).

Merry, Pippin, and Sam accompany Frodo as far as the Grey Havens, but they return back to the Shire, where they live long and useful lives.

Mayor Sam Gamgee

This is the culmination of the series of initiations that Frodo, accompanied some of the way by the other Hobbits, has undergone. First, we recall, after leaving the "ordinary" life of the Shire, comes initiation into the full, deep meaning of the physical plane of human life, shown in the trials of the Old Forest and their completion in the joy of the house of Tom Bombadil. Tom and Goldberry represent men and women of the earthly paradise, unfallen humanity in Eden naming the animals, dwellers in the Imperishable Sacred Land still preserved in Tom's corner of Middle-earth.

Then on Weathertop, Frodo is fully opened to the nature of the astral realm, the homeland of the Ring and the Nazgûl, its servants. He passes through the terror and the wounding of which its lower reaches are capable.

But at the third initiation of the Ford of Bruinen and as he enters Rivendell, Frodo glimpses the true nature of the mental plane in its nonattached beauty and intimate companionship. He now carries with him from these last two preliminary initiations a fuller realization of the dimensions of both terror and glory all around, from which both he and we are too easily cut off by the comfortable life of the Shire.

At length comes the great initiation of Mount Doom. Like the fourth initiation, it is a solitary ordeal bringing a breakthrough into the buddhic plane. This is the plane of the adept who has cleared channels to the higher Self and, through it, to cosmic consciousness. At this level one has transcended attachment to the separate individual self, which even the greatest evil magician has not forsaken. The adept of the fourth initiation therefore lives in the universe as in Nirvana, in the infinite mind of Brahman, as God who is pure love. Despite his failure to give up the Ring voluntarily, Frodo seems nonetheless to have been taken through this gateway in some manner by the awesome events at the Cracks of Doom.

However, even after such a climactic transition, one is still in the body and in the world. Earthly life is not surrendered; it is just lived in a new way. After banqueting with saints in celebration of victory, one must still do the dishes; after descending from the mountaintop of a peak experience, one must obey traffic laws. One may, like Frodo, share in triumphs and participate in the coronations of others, but the Nirvanic soul still has to come home, as the Hobbits do to the Shire, and there clean-up work remains.

The evening of Frodo's life—those last two years after Mount Doom—represents metaphorically the final embodied stage of the spiritual ascent. It is called in various traditions the unitive state, enlightenment, self-realization, immortality. The wise Flemish mystic Jan de Ruysbroeck speaks of it as wandering in a world in which the only guide is divine love. Meister Eckhart calls it knowing "God above god," the God who is everywhere and beyond all our names and concepts for God. The Buddhist Nagarjuna teaches that Nirvana cannot be known by any of the senses, for it has no color or shape, and is one and the same as Samsara, the world of everyday life.

The old Zen master Ch'ing-yuan said that before he had studied Zen, he saw mountains as mountains and streams as streams. When he had made some progress, he no longer saw mountains as mountains and streams as streams. But when he got to the very heart of Zen, he again saw mountains as mountains and streams as streams. Once when D. T. Suzuki, the great apostle of Zen to the West, told this story in a lecture, a questioner asked him about the difference between the first seeing of mountains and streams and the second. Suzuki answered, "None at all, except the second time from about two feet off the ground."

All this is telling us that, for some mystics, living in Nirvana, enlightenment, or oneness is just everyday life, and the only difference is far down within. The great contemporary American mystic of the unitive state, Bernadette Roberts (in *The Path to No-Self*), said, "On the surface of things little has changed; the transformation is not concerned with external features. The unitive state wears no particular face to the world; there is no uniform mold to which the soul conforms after its transformation. Only God and the soul know of this interior state; nothing appears of it on the outside." It is not even, she goes on to say, that such a soul is always perfect, or incapable of making mistakes of judgment or belief. The person is not a divine robot. Rather, "what is divine is the deep, interior source of acts."

Neither the Ring-bearer nor Sam become preachers of the light they have gained, as might the saint or guru of popular lore. They instead present the ideal of enlightened persons in day-by-day life, of those who are so deeply transformed that they do not need to say or do anything special to prove it, but simply are united with all that is on all planes, whatever is done or not done. This saint is like a candle in a still place, not a strobe light. Quietly effective in any helpful task that appears, that individual has the knack of being in the right place and saying the right thing without seeming effort.

So it is that Frodo and Sam—who certainly shares in whatever his master has attained—together with the other Hobbits restore the Shire. As long as the erstwhile Ring-bearer is quietly present, that domain prospers unprecedentedly, and ordinary life goes on, but with a special glow in the air.

Yet no passage through this world, however illumined, abides forever. The cycles of coming and going, the laws of necessity, apply to everyone. The Wisdom tradition does not denigrate physical existence—it rejoices in Tom Bombadil's world—but suggests there is *more* than separate physical existence as we know it here. Physical existence has no *complete* meaning without that *more*—the inner planes: etheric, astral, and mental, the buddhic plane of cosmic consciousness, the universal divine plane. We must at times be ready to give up aspects of physical life to know the inner planes better, even as an athlete in training must give up some kinds of physical indulgence in order to realize fully the potential of the physical body itself. Life and death sound the same message—we are to experience but not to hold. The day comes when we must give up separate physical existence altogether.

We might ask why we need to go through the traumas of birth and death at all. Could not nature be programmed so that an organism could simply regenerate itself over and over, without death at least so long as the universe lasts? Perhaps, and that seems to be what the Dark Lord and his Nazgûl achieve in some manner, for self-made immortality is the ultimate dream of the evil magician who combines sorcery with selfishness.

But to what point? That goal would not be serving, as physical life must, the higher purposes of life. Deathless life in this often dark world would not greatly advance the pilgrim's infinite journey through space and time or progress up the initiatory ladder of realization toward transcendence of the separate self and back to the One. That progress requires that we experience and then withdraw—that we learn *how* to withdraw and to understand *what* we have experienced, in all its ramifications and potential for the future.

That process of withdrawing and understanding of experience, according to Theosophy, is the purpose of the afterdeath working out and closing down of attachments in the astral plane, and then the assimilation experience of the mental plane, called "Devachan." To learn we must experience rebirth, life in the world, the letting go called death, the release of attachments, the Devachanic assimilation, and then rebirth again—over and over, till we finally do it all very well, and then move on to other experiences and eventually drop all that is finite. The initiations of this life are, of course, tremendously significant milestones along that great Path.

Those same initiations, on the other hand, can leave deep imprints, imprints that only the next experience of letting go and venturing to the otherworld can smooth out. Even after returning to the Shire, Frodo feels the wounds of his adventure. It is asserted that even after a Buddha's enlightenment, though his mind then has full equanimity, the results of past karma still find expression in physical suffering. Above all, he is still mortal, for a body that was karma-made has no power to endure when the karma that made it has been expended or its special purpose has been achieved.

So, as we have seen, Frodo experiences suffering on the anniversary day of his experience on Mount Doom and knows the time is fast approaching when he must leave. His embarkation from the Grey Havens is part of a larger westward movement, for it is also the end of the Third Age, an aeonic fulfillment that he himself has done more than anyone else to achieve but which means that he and his companions are of the past rather than of the future of Middle-earth.

Frodo's own spiritual growth is now to be continued on other planes. The frontier of the buddhic and divine planes, in which he can now live, is symbolized by the seamless silver curtain of rain through which he passes as his bark nears the shores of the Undying Lands and by the pervasiveness of song and perfume in the air.

The journey out of the Grey Havens takes Frodo and his party beyond the circles of this world, but not beyond life or experience. Perhaps their journey over the Sundering Sea can be understood as their rising high up on the Theosophical planes or perhaps as their transport to a realm of living legend best known to Middle-earth itself. In any case, we are the richer for the passage of the Companions of the Ring through our own consciousness. As Bilbo's departing song in the first chapter of *The Lord of the Rings* says, their lives and ours intersect in

> *. . . some wider way*
> *Where many paths and errands meet.*
> *And whither then? I cannot say.*

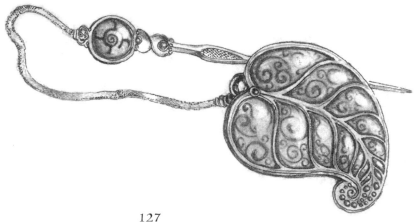

J. R. R. Tolkien, young and old, and his literary world

9

Tolkien's Quest; or, How This Book Came to Be Written

The three volumes of *The Lord of the Rings* by John Ronald Reuel Tolkien (1892–1973) have affected the inner lives of millions in the second half of the twentieth century and the beginning of the twenty-first to an extent matched by very few other works of fiction. The world of wonder, questing, self-sacrifice, and sublime values that the book evokes so unforgettably before the eye of imagination has sustained innumerable readers through times often dark and confusing in which, however, as in the days of Middle-earth, hope has never entirely vanished.

The Lord of the Rings has sold more than fifty million copies since its first publication in 1954–55. Clubs, college classes, doctoral dissertations, calendars, other books by and about Tolkien or his work have proliferated, and in 2001–03 a long-awaited movie version premiered. Surely this response betokens an immense popular yearning for a recovery of heroism in difficult yet uneasily comfortable times. We have treasured Tolkien's fictional creation of overarching meaning in the tumultuous events of history and the author's remarkable sense of transcendent beauty in nature and in simple lives.

Chapter Nine

From its beginnings in the coldest years of the Cold War, to its remarkable appeal in the radical 1960s and its success in the following decades, Tolkien's epic has kept step with the times. For not a few of its readers, *The Lord of the Rings* has had an incomparable impact on the deepest recurring images in mind and soul. Its pictures have seeped into waking and sleeping dreams, while its adventures have provided models for one's own ventures into realms of action in a world of conflict. Above all, the epic seems to inform us that our lives are lived against a mighty backdrop of cosmic purpose and splendor. Its signals tell us that though the road be hard and the stars unreachably far away, the journey can be completed, and the ring of evil broken.

I myself am one of the millions touched by Tolkien's epic. *The Lord of the Rings* has been a companion of my inner life virtually since the beginning of its own career in present-day Middle-earth. I first read the story just after it was published in 1955, when I was a student at an Episcopal seminary in New Haven, Connecticut. Tolkien's masterpiece was by no means as popular then as it would become after the publication of mass-market American paperback versions in the next decade, but the trilogy had already been discovered by the Anglophiles around my school and Yale; it was the "in" thing in those circles to read and talk about. In the summer of 1956, when I first traveled to England, I could not help but feel I was arriving at the starting point, at least, of Frodo's adventure in *The Lord of the Rings*. As I took long walks down the hedgerows of the sceptered isle's green countryside, I imagined I was walking through the Shire, with just the possibility up ahead of meeting Elves or a Wizard.

Later, my wife of more than three decades now, Gracia Fay, and I were first drawn together in part by a common love of Tolkien's epic. That was while I was in graduate school at the University of Chicago in the middle 1960s, where I lived with some other compatible students in an old rambling Victorian house. We sometimes had wonderful parties in "Toad Hall," as we called the place, where the main entertainment often was dramatic readings from *The Lord of the Rings*.

Gracia Fay herself wrote a book on the Tolkien narrative, *Good News from Tolkien's Middle Earth* (1970), which effectively interpreted the novel in terms both of parapsychology and the Christian story. In the later 1960s and early 1970s particularly, we attended meetings in the Los Angeles area of the Mythopoeic Society, a group dedicated to discussing the works of Tolkien, C. S. Lewis, and Charles Williams—three writers of common sympathies who often met around the 1940s in an Oxford pub called "The Eagle and Child" to read and talk about each other's writings.

Our Mythopoeic Society not only read aloud and talked—often at great length—but held costume parties, dramas, and conventions all based on the colorful characters of the three mythopoeic writers. Some afternoons, casual Angeleno drivers would be astonished to see a city park peopled by Hobbits, Elves, Dwarves, a Wizard or two, perhaps even a menacing Nazgûl. Those were strange sights even for the environs of Hollywood and Disneyland.

In the late 1960s, those meetings were often overflowing with denizens of the era's famed counterculture, who wore garb that was vivid and quasi-medieval enough even when they were not in costume. These long-haired and bearded apprentice Wizards and bright-eyed Elf maidens were overflowing with tales of visions and spiritual experiences that testified to firsthand encounters, at least as they understood them, with realms of mythopoeic otherness.

One might wonder exactly why the Tolkien saga, like the comparable works of Hermann Hesse, had such an appeal for the mystical outsiders of the 1960s. After all, those folk were supposed to be revolutionary levelers and people's power advocates as well as mythopoeic visionaries. Tolkien was himself far from a radical, and his story actually presents a European conservative's antiegalitarian paradise, steeped in the values of hierarchy and chivalry, full of true kings, daring knights, loyal retainers, and jolly peasants. Only when usurpers take the place of sovereigns legitimated by very long bloodlines is there trouble in his paradise. Can this be a 1960s outlook? Certainly reactionary royalism was not then taken seriously by very many as a model for governance in the present incarnation of Middle-earth.

But look at it this way. Tolkien's world bore counterculturalists (and thousands of others in the 1960s), as if on Gandalf's aerial mount Gwaihir the Windlord, far away from Vietnam and the burning streets of their America and into a marvelous realm that, in the term of the time, expanded consciousness as though the books were the Palantír. The 1960s consciousness expanders and social utopians were neoromantics. Wonder and imagination teach the romantic a profounder truth than does the pedestrian world at eye level.

Romantic wonder is aroused by deep vistas in space and time, by range after range of snowy mountains, by sky and stars, and by thoughts of kings and forgotten empires in immemorial antiquity. Romance also awakens the sweet and poignant yearning—what the Germans call *Sehnsucht*—evoked by the glimpse of distant or past marvels, even as one knows that in their fullness they are unattainable or irretrievable. Often these sentiments were induced by accounts of an idealized medieval world like Tolkien's, full of castles, knights, and epic adventure.

The heroes and villains of Middle-earth also suited the 1960s anti-establishment worldview, for Hobbits, Elves, and Wizards were no more at ease in the "plastic" modern world than were the counterculturalists. The Ring-bearers' companions of diverse kindred lived well with sun and stars and all green things, as well as with all innocent human joys. The Enemy, on the other hand, was just what many 1960s people saw as their foe in the era's social struggles: a tyrannical, inhuman, casually brutal technological order—the System, they would have called it. *The Lord of the Rings* set the regimented, robot-like slave society of Mordor against the heroic few who were friends of Elves and of starlight—a magnificent metaphor for the way many in the 1960s saw themselves ranged against the machine.

Tolkien's Quest; or, How This Book Came to Be Written

In 1973, Gracia Fay and I happened to be staying in Oxford at the time of Tolkien's death. We attended his funeral, conducted by his son John, a Roman Catholic priest. We were impressed by the smallness of the unopened casket and the simplicity of the modern rite by which he embarked from the Grey Havens for the Undying Lands. I also attended a memorial service for the writer at his Oxford college, Merton, on November 17, 1973, from which I still retain the service leaflet; the first scripture lesson contained these words from the Book of Wisdom (8.13): "Because of her [Wisdom] I shall have immortality, and leave an everlasting remembrance to those who come after me."

Shortly before he died, Tolkien had sent Gracia Fay a signed note in appreciation of her book, a rare honor for he very seldom gave out autographs despite countless requests. He commented that her name sounded Elvish.

Another even more curious item. About this time, back in southern California, we heard about a group centered around a mystical woman living in the Mojave Desert who was convinced that *The Lord of the Rings* saga was actual history, and Tolkien knew it, though for reasons the author deemed compelling he veiled the chronicle in fictional form. She had regular conversations with Elves, Dwarves, and Hobbits, and moreover was convinced that the actual site of Gondor was what is now the Mojave Desert. She believed that Aragorn's castle was buried out there, and by psychic means had determined the location of the ruins. She was continually announcing archeological excavations to be conducted by her group, then postponing the date for one reason or another. One of my students in religious studies became intrigued by this strange organization and joined it as a participant-observer, remaining until the founder finally expelled him on some pretext. But he wrote a fascinating research paper about the episode.

Chapter Nine

It was later in the 1970s that I became involved with the Wisdom tradition called Theosophy, eventually writing several books on it: *Theosophy* (1986) and *The Pilgrim Self* (1996) among others. While I certainly would not want to hold Tolkien responsible for this eventuality, I do not doubt that the sense of wonder at the vast reaches of space, time, and meaning earlier awakened by *The Lord of the Rings* also responded to the richness of the Theosophical worldview. Theosophy, as I understand it, similarly arouses an awareness of the world's mysterious gestation out of both matter and mind through the action of high intelligences: the Dhyan Chohans in Theosophy suggest the Valar in Middle-earth. In both origin stories, consciousness-like energies and their material vehicles are deeply interfused.

Moreover, in both of those worldviews, cause-and-effect patterns with sources deep in the half-forgotten past—in cooperation with our own wills—help to shape the experiences and destinies we meet now. In both, evil and good seeds planted far back in previous ages when the world was different bloom as flowers of ill or sweet odor in the present. At the same time, spores left by those who now walk the earth will break through the planet's dark soil to unfold their leaves under far future skies—call the process destiny, providence, evolution, or the harvest cycles of superior intelligences invisibly cultivating the gardens of the world.

In Tolkien's work, the Ring is the supreme token and bearer of past evil visiting the present; yet its malice is neither the end nor the ultimate beginning of the story. In the impressive words already cited, Gandalf said that in retrospect he knew Bilbo was *meant* to find the Ring, and *not* by its maker.

Another common Theosophical and Tolkienian theme is initiation. Initiation is a frequent term in Theosophy. In *The Lord of the Rings*, the reality appears, although the word does not. Theosophy talks of inner initiations conveyed through dreams and intuitions on the level of inward consciousness. As we have seen, the Ring-bearer, Frodo, passed through several ordeals of virtual death and rebirth on the way to his accomplishment of the unimaginable quest laid upon him, the destruction of the Ring that was the cynosure of evil in his age of the world.

All this does not mean that *The Lord of the Rings* is an allegory of the Ancient Wisdom or Theosophy. Tolkien himself famously disliked allegory, and refused to see his masterwork as allegorical of anything, though he did perhaps somewhat reluctantly consent to what he called "applicability."

If there are any conscious allegorical echoes in Tolkien's story, they must have to do with the main Christian drama of salvation, not surprisingly since the author was a devout Roman Catholic. To the best of my knowledge, Tolkien never discussed explicit echoes, though he did assert that *The Lord of the Rings* is a basically Christian and Catholic work. Yet it must be more than coincidence that the Ring party left Rivendell on December 25. Furthermore, the destruction of the Ring occurred on March 25, the traditional day in Western church calendars for celebrating the Annunciation of the Blessed Virgin Mary, and so of the dawning of a new spiritual age. Probably more significantly, that date also marks the approximate beginning of the season in which Holy Week and Easter can occur. Like Jesus over the few days of that week, the Ring-bearer, Frodo, was tortured, bound, abandoned, and virtually killed, before accomplishing his awesome task, the destruction of the Ring, thereby delivering a mighty blow to evil in the world.

In my enthusiasm I once voiced the opinion that *The Lord of the Rings* might provide a better mythohistorical "preparation" for the gospel of Jesus than the varied and sometimes disconcerting Christian Old Testament. I was set to rights by a scholar of the Hebrew scriptures (the Old Testament of

Christians). Though herself a Tolkien fan, she pointed out that the incomparable richness and provocative quality of the Scriptures we have lie in their inspired contributions from many hands, many spiritual points of view, and in their embeddedness in the messy realities of human history and often tragic human life as it is.

Tolkien no doubt would have agreed; he had a part in the production of the Jerusalem Bible, an ecumenical version noted especially for its literary quality, for which he Englished the Book of Job. That magnificent poem, full of anguished doubt and no less anguished faith, in a world so dark that even the goodness of God can be questioned, explores deep recesses of the human psyche untouched even by *The Lord of the Rings*, and reminds us that no one book tells all there is to tell about humanity's infinite diversity.

Yet it can hardly be denied that reading *The Lord of the Rings* has applicability to one's understanding of the mysteries of Israel and of Christ. They both show the ultimate victory of a people or a person who is obscure and seemingly of little power over the miasma of terror spread by evil's vast armies. They also show the unimaginable, unexpected joy of victory suddenly breaking through just when all seems most hopeless.

The time of *The Lord of the Rings'* writing and first release, the middle decade of the twentieth century, is also relevant. I once thought, in another odd fantasy, that it was a shame the books had not been published back in the nineteenth century, simply because I considered how much many Victorians, with their romantic love of chivalry, medievalism, and ancient lays like the tales of King Arthur and the Holy Grail, might have enjoyed *The Lord of the Rings*. Tolkien's own youthful mind was undoubtedly affected by that Victorian "return to Camelot" atmosphere.

But then I reflected that *The Lord of the Rings*, for all its patina of medieval traditionalism and even its sometimes archaic speech, is really a twentieth-century book. No doubt Victorians would have appreciated the epic, but the plot would probably never have suggested itself to most of them. Nineteenth-century romance, whether of Sir Walter Scott or Richard Wagner or Tennyson's *Idylls of the King*, was mostly about individual heroics or national mythologies set well in the past, which one could enjoy knowing they were locked securely in ages long gone. But those romances did not have the applicability of a story like Tolkien's. *The Lord of the Rings*, though putatively laid in the remote past, is in many ways all too contemporary.

The evil of Middle-earth arises in the East and is so dreadful as to threaten the world with total war and total conquest. It extends itself throughout more and more of the world by a combination of fear, force, honey-tongued propaganda, and secret collaborators in high places. It spreads terror through the skies, through networks of rumor, and by hints of the unspeakable fate of those who become its captives. Is it not to twentieth century nightmares that this terrible vision answers?

Tolkien wrote in the years before and during the greatest war in history against such a foe, whose Dark Tower was raised in a new Mordor east of England and the names of whose slave camps still raise shudders of dread. The creator of Middle-earth continued working in the early years of the Cold War, finishing the epic in the early 1950s, just after the fall of eastern Europe and of China to the influence of the Stalinist empire with its totalitarianism, gulags, and alleged subversives ensconced in the councils of folk still outside the terrible dominion's full control. At the commencement of the Korean War in 1950, all indeed seemed dark for the Western alliance of free peoples, as Tolkienesque language might have put it. It was easy to see in that world the lightning flashes of apocalyptic conflict between day and night. So it was again in the 1960s, though with the flexible applicability of myth, the identity of the children of light and the minions of darkness somewhat shifted, as we have seen.

The whole twentieth century was a time when many of the most significant books, especially those that became touchstones for the interpretation of events or situations and for deep-level influences on lives, were not "realist" novels but literary fables and fantasies. One thinks not only of J. R. R. Tolkien, Hermann Hesse, or C. S. Lewis, but also of the feverish visions of George Orwell's *Animal Farm* and *Nineteen Eighty-four*, Joseph Heller's *Catch-22*, or Franz Kafka's *The Trial*. It was as though the extremes touched by twentieth-century life could be evoked only through such media, as though those times were more like living in a myth or fantasy than in what some still insisted was the "real world." To this unorthodox canon, *The Lord of the Rings* adds an incomparable sense of "deep background" to the mysterious events of the present, as well as a sense of the supreme importance of heroism on all dimensions of reality, worthy of ancient myth even in the face of contemporary war.

Tolkien's epic has often been called a modern myth. Myth has power and may be used for good, but it is always dangerous. The myths of nations and heroes have inspired great deeds of righteousness, and no less great wickedness. The peril lies in the way myths usually oversimplify and polarize human affairs into the dichotomy of pure evil on the one hand and pure good on the other. But though very occasionally such thinking may have a place, as it may well have had when Tolkien wrote, human affairs are rarely so well defined.

The tendency, encouraged by myth, to idealize one side—usually our own—and demonize its opposite leads to the unwholesome dehumanizing of others. After the others have been made into unpersons, if not devils, persecution and even holocaust follow. Responsible and mature action in the world requires that we see ourselves and our fellow human beings for the fully rounded, incredibly complex creatures of bodies, feelings, and consciousness that we are. Most of us contain much that is good and much else that is evil, or at least not fully under control. Some critics would say responsible fiction requires no less.

Tolkien's critics have perceived flaws of this nature in his mythopoeia. They have pointed out that his characters tend to be one-dimensional, that the few female characters in particular are marginal and stereotyped, and that the story as a whole portrays a misleadingly black-and-white world, as well as one with a lot of nonsense about magic and, even more disheartening, a tendency to characterize races who have given themselves over to the service of evil as dark-skinned or "swarthy."

Of course there are occasional lapses of judgment and sensitivity in Tolkien's work, as there no doubt are in the work of many other well-known authors. But it is important to realize what kind of book *The Lord of the Rings* is. It is not the how-we-live-now kind of novel that paints of life in our own boardrooms and bedrooms, animated by people we meet on the street and see in the mirror.

Tolkien, who did not write realist novels, gave himself the last word against his critics, as was his right. In the foreword to the second edition of *The Lord of the Rings*, he wrote that he had no desire to protest the opinions of those of his reviewers who found the story ridiculous or "contemptible," since he had no higher view of their books or of the sort of books they seemed to like better (xiv). A writer with opinions like these does not hold the mirror up to our everyday life. He rather holds up the mirror to our archetypes, to the image of the essential, unvarnished nature at the core of each of us, wherever we are now in our pilgrimage.

Mythmakers are aware that beneath everything else, we are archetypal selves—caught in a self-portrait that, by a simple timeless image, sums up one's self or an important aspect of one's self (for there can be several archetypes in a person). If one aspires to be a scientist, it is the picture somewhere at the back of the mind of the dedicated scientist standing white-coated in the laboratory, pure and sincere in the quest for knowledge and on fire with the excitement of discovery. If one is a mother, it is the timeless mother with the child at her breast, the two alone as though surrounded by a circle of light and the only beings in the universe, yet complete.

The archetypal self is like a snapshot that makes family and friends say, "This is really Uncle Joe," or "That's the very image of Aunt Gladys." Though the certain smile caught in the photograph may be flashed only occasionally, somehow more than any other expression it *is* the real him or her. It captures an essential archetype hidden beneath the everydayness of Uncle Joe or Aunt Gladys, and lets that inner person meet the world. Archetypal writing is effective when its story makes real the wink, the gesture, or the laugh that cousins and lovers would know *is* that person deep down, even if it would take all the words in Shakespeare to tell why. In fantasy writing, in which all characters are likely to be archetypal in the sense that they embody

single, clear, and unforgettable qualities— the tenacity of Dwarves, the heroism of warriors, the earthiness of Hobbits—the writer's challenge is to make us feel that something archetypal in us corresponds to that archetype.

In one of your archetypal selves, you may be hiding a Hobbit, a Dwarf, an Elf, a Wizard, or—God forbid—a Black Rider, just as in your outer social self you may well be one of those confused and complex persons known to the "realist" novel. But in reading Tolkien, you allow that inner archetypal self, the self of hidden fantasies and forgotten dreams, to take wing in a kingdom of its own and of beings like itself, in which your own Elves sing and warriors fight courageously, and you live in realms of splendor where hopes come true.

Although there are now billions of people on this burdened planet, many times that number of selves inhabit its inner spaces of dreams, archetypes, and marvels. The popularity of Tolkien's mythic novel, *The Lord of the Rings*, attests to their reality. This vast epic was really written for those invisible readers, who must use our eyes to see into their world.

Appendix A:

Synopsis of *The Hobbit* and *The Lord of the Rings*

The first book of the Ring series, *The Hobbit* (1937), tells us that one day to the door of Bilbo, a Hobbit, there comes the Wizard Gandalf and thirteen Dwarves. They request him to accompany them on a quest for great treasure belonging to the Dwarf King under the Mountain, but now held by the dragon Smaug. After reluctantly undertaking this task, Bilbo becomes lost on the way after an attack by Orcs in the Misty Mountains and finds himself deep in caverns beneath the range. There he finds a ring on the floor of a tunnel. After putting it in his pocket, he encounters Gollum, the miserable creature who regards that ring as his "Precious," the one thing he loves.

Gollum challenges Bilbo to a riddle-game, saying that if the Hobbit cannot guess the answers, he will kill and eat him, but if he can, he will show him the way out of the caverns. In the end Bilbo wins by asking the question "What do I have in my pocket?" which the other is unable to answer. The Hobbit is able to escape with the ring, which he soon learns will make him invisible. But when Gollum discovers it missing, and realizes what his adversary had in his pocket, he vows eternal hatred of Bilbo.

Rejoining his party, Bilbo is able to assist the Dwarves to defeat the Orcs in the Battle of Five Armies, as well as destroy the dragon and recover the treasure. He then returns to Hobbiton, keeping the ring, secured by a fine chain, in his pocket.

Appendix A

The Fellowship of the Ring

The first volume of *The Lord of the Rings* begins in the Shire, the homeland of the Hobbits, with Bilbo's birthday party sixty years after the events of *The Hobbit*, when he is 111. His nephew Frodo (who has the same birthday, and is now coming of age at 33) has become Bilbo's heir. Gandalf in the meantime has come to suspect that Bilbo's ring is the One Ring, ruler of all the Rings of Power. At the party, Bilbo puts on the Ring, disappears, and slips away to join the Elves at Rivendell. With some hesitation, but at Gandalf's insistence, he passes the Ring on to Frodo.

Some seventeen years later, Gandalf calls on Frodo to confirm his suspicion about the Ring, also telling Frodo that he is in great danger from the Dark Lord of Mordor, Sauron. That evil being's Black Riders are searching for the Ring, which will complete their master's power. Knowing that he must leave the Shire to keep that peaceful land and the Ring safe from the forces of darkness, Frodo, accompanied by his faithful retainer, Sam, and two younger Hobbits, Merry and Pippin, departs for Rivendell, the Last Homely House of the Elves. The Hobbits first enter the perilous Old Forest, where they are rescued by Tom Bombadil. Stopping at the Inn at Bree, they are joined by the Ranger called Strider. On the dangerous journey from there to Rivendell, the Black Riders succeed in piercing Frodo with a poisonous dagger but do not gain the Ring. After another close escape at the Ford of Bruinen, the party arrives at Rivendell.

In Rivendell, at the Council of Elrond, it is decided that the Ring must be destroyed; this can only be done at the Cracks of Doom in the land of Mordor, where it had been made. Frodo accepts the dread mission. He sets out, accompanied by his original three Hobbit companions, by two men, Strider and Boromir, a proud warrior from Gondor (the ancient kingdom in the front line of defense against the Dark Lord), by the Dwarf Gimli, the Elf

Legolas, and Gandalf the Wizard. The Nine Walkers make their way far south until, defeated by the snowy mountain Caradhras, they enter the Gate of Moria to attempt a dangerous passage under the range. There Gandalf, battling with a powerful underworld being, the Balrog, falls into an abyss and appears to have been lost. Under the leadership of Strider, also called Aragorn, the remainder of the party emerge on the other side of the mountain and visit the mystical Elven realm of Lothlórien and its goddess-like Queen, Galadriel.

Upon leaving that land almost out of time, the companions reach the great river and approach the frontiers of Mordor. But there they separate into smaller parties. Boromir attempts to wrest the Ring from Frodo, but is rebuffed and soon after is killed by Orcs. Frodo, realizing that he must now proceed alone, puts on the Ring of invisibility and takes a boat for the other shore, but is joined at the last minute by Sam. The two young Hobbits, Merry and Pippin, are captured by Orcs, and the remaining three companions, Aragorn, Legolas, and Gimli, pursue those goblins into the Kingdom of Rohan, the land of horse riders.

The Two Towers

The second book in the series describes the subsequent adventures of the divided members of the Ring party. The two captured Hobbits, Merry and Pippin, eventually escape and enter the realm of the Ents, tree-like intelligent beings of great age. Aragorn, Gimli, and Legolas come to the court of the aged king of Rohan, Theoden. He is under the control of Wormtongue, a counselor in league with the fallen Wizard, Saruman.

But Gandalf returns from apparent death to heal Theoden and inspire him to lead his forces against those of Saruman. The riders of Rohan prevail at the battle of Helm's Deep as the Ents destroy Isengard, the stronghold of Saruman. Merry and Pippin are met there, and all proceed to Minas Tirith, the great fortress-city of Gondor. War with the armies of Sauron, led by the Nazgûl, the former Black Riders now mounted on nightmarish winged creatures, is clearly imminent.

In the meantime, Frodo and Sam wander through the bleak hills of Emyn Muil. They meet Gollum, whom they compel to become their guide. He leads them through Ithilien, where they come upon a party of Gondorian troops led by Faramir, brother of Boromir. Gollum then takes them into the passageway of Cirith Ungol. In it they confront the evil giant spider Shelob, who captures and paralyzes Frodo, forcing Sam to vanquish her and briefly carry the Ring. His master's inert form is taken by Orcs, but Sam rescues him from them also. After Frodo recovers, he, Sam, and Gollum as unwilling guide are ready for the last march to the Cracks of Doom.

The Return of the King

In this final volume, we learn first of the desperate state of Gondor under its Steward, Denethor, successor of a long and proud line that has ruled that land since the time of its last king long ago. But the aging custodian of the realm has fallen into hopelessness. As the Enemy lays siege, Denethor prepares his own funeral pyre. Gondor and the West appear about to be overwhelmed by the vast forces of the Dark Lord.

At the same time, Frodo and his companions are continuing to progress through the Dark Land to Mount Doom and the Cracks of Doom, despite extreme fatigue, hunger, and thirst. But upon finally reaching it, Frodo, completely under the Ring's power by now, refuses to destroy the Ring but instead puts it on. However, Gollum wrestles it from him, biting off the former Ring-bearer's finger, and holding it high topples into the Cracks of Doom, annihilating both himself and his "Precious."

At the destruction of the Ring, the power of the Dark Lord is broken. Leaderless, his armies flee. Aragorn, who has been revealed to be the rightful king, is crowned as King Elessar of Gondor and the North. Frodo and the other Hobbits return to the Shire in a leisurely progress, visiting Rohan, Isengard, Rivendell, and other sites of their earlier adventures. Upon arriving at the Shire, however, they find it fallen under harsh masters ultimately controlled by Saruman. The returning Hobbits restore their homeland's proper order, and the Shire enjoys seasons of wonderful abundance and peace.

But the following year Frodo is joined by Gandalf, Galadriel, and Bilbo. Knowing their time in Middle-earth is over and their work ended with the end of the Third Age, they all proceed to the Grey Havens, where they set sail for the Undying Lands.

Appendix B:

The Inner Planes

This summary, adapted from that in the author's book *The Cross and the Grail*, is offered for the benefit of readers who may not be familiar with the Theosophical concept of inner planes of human and universal reality.

The Theosophical interpretation of esoteric wisdom demarcates seven "planes" within a human being and in the universe as a whole. Accounts vary in some details; the following is the schema used in *Frodo's Quest*. Here the seven are the physical plane, the etheric plane, the astral or feeling and desire plane, the lower mental plane, the upper mental plane, the buddhic or intuitive and cosmic consciousness plane, and the inmost divine plane. The individual and universal aspects of each are distinct, yet intersect and interact on deep levels, just as our physical body is clearly distinguishable from the rest of the universe yet is also an inseparable part of it. The inner planes make up, as it were, the continuum between the individual in the physical body and universal divine reality.

The use of the word "planes" is only a metaphor, as are other terms sometimes used, such as "sheaths," "spheres," or "bodies." They are not actually stacked on top of each other or one inside the other like a Russian babushka doll, but interpenetrate or coexist in the same space at the same time, just as oxygen can exist in water and water in a sponge, because of varying degrees of fineness of the "matter" in the different substances. Reality is always mutlilayered, even as it appears to be in Middle-earth. Just as the skin, flesh, and bones of a physical body are all equally real, so are the physical, emotional, mental, intuitive, and pure consciousness levels of existence, both personal and universal.

The seven planes are divided into the lower quaternity and the higher triad. The lower quaternity includes first the physical body. The etheric level, the next plane, surrounds the body like an energy field, providing a mold or model for the body. Then comes the astral or emotional body, based on desire. Many dreams and fantasies, both sleeping and waking, are astral plane activities. Discarnate beings like the Black Riders on the astral plane can and do interact with those inner visions, infecting us with desires and providing opportunities for their fulfillment in reverie, or even in out-of-body experiences. Though most astral thoughts and astral-plane beings are needy in some way, requiring caution and compassion, not everything on the astral level is actively bad; great concepts and works of art, though still desire-centered, can come out of its highest reaches.

The mental body is on a more refined level than the astral, comprising not desire-based thoughts, but rather thoughts that are the seeds of creativity and grand in scope, encompassing vast ranges of understanding. This level, the mental plane, is also the after-death state called "Devachan"; here entities rest and, on the basis of karma, gather seed-thoughts that provide deep motifs for their next lives. Devachan corresponds to the common idea of heaven.

As we enjoy physical existence here in this world, we are actually living in all seven planes at once. But it is not necessary for consciousness to have a physical component. The inner consciousness of an individual, centered in the mental planes, can separate from the lower spheres: physical, etheric, and astral. Indeed, that is said to happen to all of us at death. First the etheric body, carrying the other inner planes within it, departs from the physical remains. Next the etheric falls away, leaving us in the astral realm of dreams and desires, as Frodo was when wearing the Ring. This was also the world the Ring's twisted servants knew. Finally, when all dreams and desires are played out, the astral sphere may dissolve, leaving us in the mental and higher realms only. On it the lessons of the past life are assimilated until it is time to reenter physical existence again, if that is one's destiny.

The mental level is twofold. On the lower mental plane, thoughts are concrete and employ forms and images, though not desire-based ones. The upper mental plane is mind beyond the level of form and image as we know it, being sweeping and universal; in it concepts such as love, power, or reality are themselves concrete realities.

The divide between the lower and upper mental planes is also the divide between the lower quaternity and the higher triad. Still above the upper mental plane in the triad is the buddhic or intuitive level, where thought transcends the separate individual self altogether to merge into cosmic consciousness or universal awareness. This level is beyond the range of the evil magician, who thinks only of power for the self. Still beyond, or within, the buddhic is Atma, the Brahmanic or Divine consciousness, which makes of that universality the conscious awareness of an infinite divine mind.

Appendix C:

The "Root Races" and Ancient Ages

In its many different forms, the Ancient Wisdom views the history of life on this planet as twofold: it has an inner, consciousness-based line of evolution, and also the bodily evolution described by paleontology and physical anthropology. The twain did not come together to form proto-humans until relatively recently by evolutionary standards. Moreover, the emergence of consciousness is sorted out into great periods or ages, each with its particular emphasis and each also coming to an appropriately dramatic ending.

Even as *The Lord of the Rings* divides history into three ages, with Gandalf's work specifically in the Third, so Theosophy divides the story of the line of consciousness leading to present human life on this earth into the times of various "Root Races," of which the present is the fifth. Each Root Race had a "continent" or landmass associated with it. Most Theosophists take the Root Races to refer to stages in the evolution of consciousness, not to races in the popular physical sense.

The first two and a half Root Races did not have fully physical bodies but lived only on the inner astral or etheric planes (see appendix B for a discussion of these planes) rather than in solid flesh like ours. The continent of the first Root Race, called the "Imperishable Sacred Land," seems rather like

Tolkien's Valinor, a part of the Undying Lands beyond the Sundering Sea, inhabited by immortal High Elves.

About halfway through the time of the third Root Race, some spiritually evolved beings called "the Lords of the Flame" arrived on Earth to assist the conjoining of the two lines of evolution—the mental and astral of the first and second Root Races with physical forms presumably from out of Darwinian animal evolution. This third Root Race, called "Lemurian" (a term taken from nineteenth-century science) perhaps corresponds anthropologically to protohuman primates and Paleolithic humans. Like the first men in Middle-earth, the Lemurians built simple but monumental cities, and their times were beset by good and evil magic.

The fourth Root Race, the Atlantean (taking its name from the Platonic myth), resembled the Tolkienesque men of Númenor. They dwelt in a now-lost land that rose to great magnificence, but finally descended into the sea as a result of pride, evil magic, and an attempt to try the power of the Guardians themselves. The last king of the Númenoreans, tempted by Sauron, had dared to break the Ban of the Valar and sail to the Undying Lands, whose bright shores were then visible from Númenor, though forbidden. But when the presumptuous intruders set foot on the Shores of the Blessed, the earth changed. Númenor sank, Valinor and Elvenhome were forever removed from the circles of this world, and the Second Age came to an end.

So also, according to Theosophical sources, the sinking of Atlantis marked the end of the fourth and the beginning of the fifth Root Race, our own. (Atlantis refers to a stage of consciousness and does not necessarily imply the existence of a physical island of Atlantis.) In our time, magic and psychic power—access to other worlds—are much more closed off than before. It is our Root Race's particular calling to explore the material plane, for which scientific and technological means are especially appropriate, and that we have done.

Each of the Root Races is said to be under the worldly leadership of an adept called the Manu, and the spiritual guidance of a Buddha. The holders of these offices, with their companions and students, change from one such era to another, the Manu and Buddha of each Root Race being apprentices during the previous age. The role of these figures is similar to that of Tolkien's Wizards, as protectors and guides.

Selected References

Books by J. R. R. Tolkien

The Hobbit; or, There and Back Again. London: Allen and Unwin, 1937.

The Lord of the Rings. 3 parts: *The Fellowship of the Ring; The Two Towers; The Return of the King.* London: Allen and Unwin, 1954–5.

The Silmarillion. London: Allen and Unwin, 1977.

Books about Tolkien and His Works

Bloom, Harold, ed. *J. R. R. Tolkien.* Philadelphia: Chelsea House Publishers, 2000.

Carpenter, Humphrey. *Tolkien: A Biography.* Boston: Houghton Mifflin, 1977.

Chance, Jane. *The Lord of the Rings: The Mythology of Power.* New York: Twayne Publishers, 1992.

Clark, George, and Daniel Timmons, eds. *J. R. R. Tolkien and His Literary Resonances: Views of Middle-earth.* Westport, CT: Greenwood Press, 2000.

Colebatch, H. K. *Return of the Heroes: The Lord of the Rings, Star Wars and Contemporary Culture.* Perth, Australia: Australian Institute for Public Policy, 1990.

Curry, Patrick. *Defending Middle-earth: Tolkien, Myth and Modernity.* New York: St. Martin's, 1997.

Day, David. *Tolkien: The Illustrated Encyclopedia*. New York: Macmillan, 1991.

Ellwood, Gracia Fay. *Good News from Tolkien's Middle Earth*. Grand Rapids, MI: Eerdmans, 1970.

Flieger, Verlyn. *A Question of Time: J. R. R. Tolkien's Road to Faërie*. Kent, OH: Kent State University Press, 1997.

Helms, Randel. *Tolkien's World*. Boston: Houghton Mifflin, 1974.

Lobdell, Jared. *England and Always: Tolkien's World of the Rings*. Grand Rapids, MI: Eerdmans, 1981.

Noel, Ruth S. *The Mythology of Middle-earth*. Boston: Houghton Mifflin, 1977.

Pearce, Joseph. *Tolkien: Man and Myth*. San Francisco: Ignatius Press, 1998.

Petty, Anne C. *One Ring to Bind Them All: Tolkien's Mythology*. University, AL: University of Alabama Press, 1979.

Purtill, Richard. *J. R. R. Tolkien: Myth, Morality, and Religion*. San Francisco: Harper & Row, 1984.

Shippey, T. A. *J. R. R. Tolkien: Author of the Century*. London: Harper Collins, 2000.

————. *The Road to Middle-earth*. Boston: Houghton Mifflin, 1982.

Tyler, J. E. A. *The New Tolkien Companion*. New York: St. Martin's, 1979.

Books about Theosophy

Blavatsky, Helena Petrovna. *The Key to Theosophy*. Ed. Joy Mills. Wheaton, IL: Theosophical Publishing House, 1972.

————. *The Secret Doctrine*. 3 vols. Wheaton, IL: Theosophical Publishing House, 1993.

————. *The Voice of the Silence*. Wheaton, IL: Theosophical Publishing House, 1992.

Ellwood, Robert. *The Cross and the Grail*. Wheaton, IL: Theosophical Publishing House, Quest Books, 1997.

————. *The Pilgrim Self*. Wheaton, IL: Theosophical Publishing House, Quest Books, 1996.

————. *Theosophy*. Wheaton, IL: Theosophical Publishing House, Quest Books, 1986.

Hodson, Geoffrey. *The Kingdom of the Gods*. Adyar, Madras, India: Theosophical Publishing House, 1966.

Leadbeater, Charles W. *The Masters and the Path*. Adyar, Madras, India: Theosophical Publishing House, 1925.

The Mahatma Letters to A. P. Sinnett from the Mahatmas M. and K. H. Comp. A. T. Barker. Ed. Vincente Hao Chin. Manila, Philippines: Theosophical Publishing House, 1993.

Olcott, Henry S. *Old Diary Leaves*. Vol. 1. Adyar, Madras, India: Theosophical Publishing House, 1974.

Other Works Cited

Jung, Carl G. "The Meaning of Psychology for Modern Man." In *Civilization in Transition*, 134–56. New York: Pantheon, 1964.

Roberts, Bernadette. *The Path to No-Self*. Albany: State University of New York Press, 1991.

QUEST BOOKS

are published by

The Theosophical Society in America,

Wheaton, Illinois 60189-0270,

a branch of a world fellowship,

a membership organization

dedicated to the promotion of the unity of

humanity and the encouragement of the study of

religion, philosophy, and science, to the end that

we may better understand ourselves and our place in

the universe. The Society stands for complete

freedom of individual search and belief.

For further information about its activities,

write, call 1-630-668-1571, e-mail olcott@theosmail.net

or consult its Web page: http://www.theosophical.org

The Theosophical Publishing House

is aided by the generous support of

THE KERN FOUNDATION,

a trust established by Herbert A. Kern

and dedicated to Theosophical education.